God Is Not Fair, He Is More Than Fair

Walking with God through the storms of life

By: Lee E. Pollock

Copyright © 2012 by Lee E. Pollock

God Is Not Fair, He Is More Than Fair
Walking With God Through The Storms Of Life
by Lee E. Pollock

Printed in the United States of America

ISBN 9781625092311

All rights reserved solely by the author. The author guarantees all contents are original and do not infringe upon the legal rights of any other person or work. No part of this book may be reproduced in any form without the permission of the author. The views expressed in this book are not necessarily those of the publisher.

Unless otherwise indicated, Bible quotations are taken from The New International Version of the Bible. Copyright © 1973, 1978, 1984 by International Bible Society.

www.xulonpress.com

What People Are Saying About God Is Not Fair, He Is More Than Fair

"If your life situations are seemingly overwhelming and confusing; if you're not certain whether or not God is even paying attention to you and your struggles.....then you need to read this book. Lee Pollock has done an excellent job of capturing a wide range of true-life experiences from individuals and couples who have discovered in their hard places-"God isn't fair; He is more than fair!". . . . .Wayne Mueller, Asst. Dakota District Superintendent, Wesleyan Church

"Lee Pollock has a way of sharing personal stories that brings them to life on the pages of this book. If you ever doubted that God can work in all avenues of life this book will inspire you and help you believe and worship a God who is concerned about all of life.". . . . .Wayne Richards, Education and Clergy Development Division, Wesleyan Church Headquarters

"Every person needs to be lifted on the wings of hope and inspiration. This book takes life's pain and problems and carries them through the hope and inspiration that comes through faith. Through the pages of this book you will be able to walk with a variety of people and learn about their most painful experiences and see how they were able to take the golden thread of hope to make a garment of peace and comfort. You can do it too! Read and be inspired!". . ..Joe W. Colaw, Pastor of First Wesleyan Church, Bartlesville, OK.

"The details of your life really matter! This book documents how even the smallest, often overlooked detail, can become a carefully crafted tool in God's hands. It will inspire you to believe when you want to give up, to discover God's subtle interventions, and to gain a new perspective during unsettling circumstances. Since God even knows the number of hairs on your head, He certainly cares about your storm, too! He will show up in a "more than fair" miraculous kind of way!". . . Dawn Marie Colaw, MS, Certified Life Coach & Counselor

Contents

Acknowledgments ix
1. A Year Like Job's 11
2. When God Speaks, Even the Courts Listen 22
3. Plucked From the Fire 45
4. Have Your Way, Lord! 65
5. It's All Worth It 85
6. Potholes of Life 100
7. In The Shelter of His Wings 119
8. Guiding Light 135
9. Divine Appointment 153
10. In The Name of Jesus, Live! 168
11. Meanwhile Back at Chappelle 187
12. God's Way 203
13. It Is All A Matter Of Focus 219

14. Lasting Peace 231
15. Jesus Loves Even Me 248
16. Bootstrap Mentality 261
17. One In A Million 277
18. Faith Builds Faith 294
19. Only The Artist Knows 308

Acknowledgments

I would like to thank all those who made this book possible.

Thank you, my LORD and God, who called me to write this book and inspired me to keep going even when the going got ruff. Lord you never gave up on me even when I put this off for many years at a time.

Thank you, my wonderful wife Linda, who spent hundreds of hours transcribing each testimony word for word so that I could have something to write from. Linda your love for our Lord and your dedication to this work kept me going.

Thank you, Joy Kear, who put in countless hours rewriting this book, so others, would find it an enjoyable experience.

Thank you, Patricia Anderson, who also put in countless hours correcting punctuation and grammar, all for the love of our Lord.

Thank you, Dave Miller, who put me in contact with so many people with so many wonderful testimonies of what the Lord had done in their lives.

A great big thank you to everyone who shared their testimonies with me and allowed me to use them in this book.

Thank you to everyone who listened to me go on and on about the wonderful testimonies that the Lord had given me.

And, thank you to all those who read the manuscript and commented.

1

A Year Like Job's

*I*n the book of Job, Satan is given permission from God to do anything he wishes to Job, other than taking his life. So Satan took everything that Job had: his crops, his livestock, and even his children. Then to make matters worse, Satan attacked Job with a terrible case of boils from his head to his feet.

Some theologians do not believe the account of Job truly happened. A pastor friend of mine told me, that one of his ministry professors, said the book of Job was just a nice story, that is that it is a work of fiction. The professor explained that no one could have gone through all the things

Job did, and lived. If we are truly following the Lord, we can handle anything that comes our way, with Him.

There is a closeness to God that a child of God feels, when he/she is under attack by Satan. In the book of Job, when Satan enters, God asks him if he has noticed His servant, Job. I believe the Lord is just like any parent and is proud of His children. He knew how Job would handle the situation, and He proved it by letting Satan have his way, as He does in many of our lives.

In 1993-1994, our family experienced a year that one might say was a year like Job's.

It all started in November of 1993, when my mother-in-law passed away. She had been fighting cancer for several years, and lost the battle. We went to Torrington, Wyoming, where Gerald and Lola had lived for many years. Lola had not wanted a funeral, and that seemed to make our time of grieving somewhat harder.

Then, in January of 1994, Linda's dad, Gerald, called to tell us that his cancer had worsened. His doctor had given him six weeks to live. This was a hard blow, as my wife, Linda, was much closer to her dad. Also, our son took this very hard. First he lost his grandmother, and now his grandfather was dying. I'm sure he felt that his world was coming apart, which brought on a time of rebellion. In some ways, he is still in that rebellion today, against the Lord. The good thing is that Gerald's treatment was on the cutting edge of technology, and he lived another seven years. He had gone to a different doctor, who tried a new type of chemotherapy. So, for seven years, each time the cancer flared up, there was a new type of chemo. Of course, at the time, we did not know that this would be the case, so we continued in stress mode.

In February, my mother was hospitalized, the cause of which I do not know today, but I remember thinking, "Not another thing". After all, how much can a person handle before they break? We found it was a lot more than what we had already experienced, for this was just the beginning of our year. The stress would increase as life unfolded. God says to lean on Him, and not our own understanding; this was a lesson we would begin to learn, as the year went on.

In March, on the night of the high school prom, our house burned to the ground. I had the glorious pleasure of spending 12 days in the burn unit of the University of Utah Hospital, in Salt Lake City, Utah.

I will spend another chapter speaking about this time in our lives, but just let me say that it was quite different than anything I had ever experienced, before or since. I was the only one to be burned, but I had to leave the family at home, while I was there. We were separated for almost two weeks, which was hard on both them and me.

In April, my mother was back in the hospital again. At some point, a person would ask themselves if there was ever going to be an end to all of this mental pain we were experiencing, but it did not end there.

In May, I was back in the hospital. This time, I required surgery. While they were taking chest x-rays of me in the burn unit, because of the smoke I had inhaled, the doctors found that I had a Para Esophageal Hiatal Hernia. That is to say, that my stomach had made a second hole in my diaphragm, and was actually in my chest. The doctors told me that I needed to get this fixed as soon as possible, because there was a possibility that, if my stomach rolled, it could cut off the blood supply to my heart. This, in turn, would be the end of me. Pass me a little more stress, please.

You must be wondering if all this would ever end; I was. But in July, mom was back in the hospital again, and we were very worried about her. After all, this was the third time, in a matter of a few months, and it made us wonder what was going on here. You might even say, "Why are you doing this to us, Lord?" But God does not do things to us; He allows things to happen, to grow us into who He wants us to be. But even with this, we had a little more to go through.

When our daughter was born, she suffered a bleed in her head; this caused her to develop hydrocephalous, which we used to call "water on the brain". The doctors put a shunt in her brain to drain off the excess water. This had become plugged, and had to be replaced in August. It was frightening at first because the doctors could not tell what was wrong. She was fourteen at the time, so the previous shunt had lasted a lot longer than it was designed to. But now she was going blind, and no one could tell us why. We took her to another doctor, who, by looking in her eyes, could tell what the problem was. He did surgery, replacing the original shunt, and she was on her way to recovery. She is now thirty, and will be having her second child soon. Her eyesight came back, except for her peripheral vision. **God is good!**

Bringing an end to an interesting year, in September, we were told that I need to take blood thinners for the rest of my life. This is the same stuff that is used to kill mice and rats; it's called Warfarin. It seems that I had developed a condition that causes me to get blood clots, and the Warfarin, which would cause a mouse or rat to bleed to death, is the thing that will keep me alive.

A year like this would cause a lot of people in our world to throw up their hands in disgust and say that God is not fair. To this, I would agree, but in a different way. That is to say, that I do not believe that God is unfair, but He is more than fair. Fair is a word that says, whatever one gets in life is a result of what he or she does, or does not do.

In other words, we get what we deserve, but God at times circumvents this, and steps in when we do not deserve it.

Let me illustrate this with something that happened to me the other day. A group of us were riding our ATVs through the woods of the Black Hills of South Dakota. I was second to last in a line of nine ATVs; as we rode along we made several creek crossings. On two of these crossings, I had felt my ATV start to die, but then it started to run again. But on the way out, it died in the middle of the creek, and fair would have meant that I had to get myself out, on my own.

There I was, sitting in the middle of this creek, with water running over my feet, when Matt came around me, hooked on to my ATV, and began to pull me out. He not only pulled me out of the stream, but continued to pull me up the trail. After a while, my ATV started, and I was able to drive myself down the trail again. We crossed the creek, and I made it through the creek two more times, without any trouble.

On the return trip, my ATV died in the middle of the creek again. Fair would be that I would get off the ATV, wade through the water, and get myself out. But God is more than fair, sending Matt around me again, to hook on to my ATV and pull me out. Only this time, Matt's ATV couldn't pull me up the bank of the creek. Fair would have been for him to say, "Well, I tried," and be done with it. But instead, Sam took his turn pulling me out. This time, Sam pulled me clear to the top of the hill!

At the top of the hill, I was able to start my ATV again, and drive the rest of the way to where we had parked the pickups. I could still have been in the middle of that creek, with water flowing over my shoes. But people stepped in, and made it possible for me to get back to where I needed to be. This is the same way God acts at times. He will step in and get us out of a situation we have gotten ourselves into. Maybe, we get there because of something we have done, or maybe, it was just an accident. But at times, God will step into a situation, and even set aside the "laws of nature" for His children.

God Is Not Fair, He Is More Than Fair

That is not to say that the Lord will always step in, and bail us out of our circumstances. Let me illustrate this for you. On the way home from camp, I ruined the motor in our pickup. It was a diesel, and we were pulling our trailer up a steep hill. It appeared that we blew the head gasket, lost our coolant, and overheated the motor. There was no place to pull off, as there was no shoulder, so we had to go over the top of the hill to find a pull out. It could have happened where there was room to pull off, but it didn't. So, there we sat, stranded on the Crow Reservation. Had it happened in a better spot, maybe I could have saved the motor.

People began to stop and offer us help, which was really appreciated. Some gave us antifreeze for the pickup; others gave us water. One man sent his friend, who is a mechanic, out to help us. He tried, but was unable to fix the pickup. We met a lot of good people, even though we were not able to get it going again. In the end, we had to call a tow truck, to take us to the next big town.

God could have kept us from having this problem, but He chose not to. Maybe, because we needed to see that there are a lot of good people out there. Another possibility might be that we were able to help out the mechanic, with a few dollars. We may never know the reason why, but what I do know is that my God is able. I know, when He moves, great things happen, things that are not possible, without Him.

There will be more times in life when God does not step in, than times He does. Even when God doesn't choose to move, He always has what is best for His children in mind. We may not understand it, but this is where faith comes in.

True faith does not believe that God will give us this or that. It does not believe that, if we have enough faith, He will provide what we pray for. No, true faith believes that whatever God sends our way is what is best for us at the time. It believes that He is there with us through the thick and thin of life.

The apostle Paul found that God's grace is sufficient for our needs. 2 Corinthians 12:7-10, says:

> To keep me from becoming conceited because of these surpassingly great revelations, there was given me a thorn in my flesh, a messenger of Satan, to torment me. Three times I pleaded with the Lord to take it away from me. But he said to me, "My grace is sufficient for you, for my power is made perfect in weakness." Therefore I will boast all the more gladly about my weaknesses, so that Christ's power may rest on me. That is why, for Christ's

sake, I delight in weaknesses, in insults, in hardships, in persecutions, in difficulties. For when I am weak, then I am strong.

That is to say that, at times, God will leave us in our circumstances, so that we will learn to trust in Him even more. For trusting in God is knowing whatever He allows to happen in our life, is what is best for us, at the time.

This book contains a collection of testimonies of what God has done in my life, and in the lives of others I have come to know. It is my hope that by reading this, your faith will grow, as you see what the Lord has done in the lives of many people.

Things to Ponder

1. How do you define fair?
2. Is God fair in your opinion?
3. Are the stories contained in the Bible true or are they just "nice stories?"
4. Is it important to know that God is with you through "the thick and thin of life"?
5. When God does not provide what you think you need, how do you feel?

2

When God Speaks, Even the Courts Listen

*F*rom the beginning of time, God has spoken to His creation. In fact, He spoke His creation into existence. Imagine God speaking, and stars, hundreds of times larger than our earth, are created. Animals and plants suddenly appear on the earth, the sun and the moon were created and everything was good. Then He created Adam and Eve and placed them in the Garden of Eden. He walked with them and told them how to live. He told them not to eat of the fruit of the tree of the knowledge of good and evil, but they chose not to obey. Then He banished them from Eden, so they could not eat of the tree of life, and live forever in sin.

Later on, after Cain murdered his brother, Abel, God asked Cain where Abel was, although He already knew what Cain had done. He spoke to Noah and told him to build an ark to carry him and his family, for God was going to flood the earth. He spoke to Moses and sent him to rescue the people of Israel. Then, in the wilderness, He spoke, and the people became very frightened, so God stopped speaking to people in an audible voice, for the most part.

God has always spoken, and will always speak, to the hearts of people. He has placed within each and every person a conscience, so that we will know when we do wrong. He speaks to people through prayer, and He speaks to people through a still, small voice, in their hearts. The trouble is that a lot of people do not listen to this voice very well, but God will always accomplish what He wants, for there is no stopping God. The following is just one example of a person listening to the voice of God.

I first heard about Jessica Welty's story when her sister, Anna, was at our church, to share about her call to be a missionary to the Far East. It was actually Jessica and Anna's mother, Laura, who told me about Jessica. God had given me the idea for this book several years ago, and He had impressed on my heart that now was the time to write it. I told Laura about the book, and she told me that her daughter had a testimony about what God had done in her life. My wife and I were planning a trip to Bartlesville, Oklahoma, the next week, which is where Jessica lives, so a visit with Jessica was added to our plans.

It is always great to see the Hand of the Lord in our lives, and this was one of those occasions. There are no coincidences, when a person walks with the Lord. God allows, and even brings things into our lives, so that He can accomplish the things He desires. Here I was, still taking my sweet time getting around to working on this book, when He said, "Here is the next chapter." It was no coincidence that we were going to Bartlesville, it was no coincidence that Jessica lived there, and it was even no coincidence that we heard about her. We just needed to let God move in this situation. Sometimes, I think we just need to get out of God's way, and yield to Him.

So, with all that out of the way, here is Jessica's story: Jessica grew up in Sheridan, Wyoming, and then attended Oklahoma Wesleyan University, in Bartlesville, Oklahoma. She dated a man named Russ, all through her years in college; they married and stayed in Bartlesville. One night, Russ suggested that they have a family who lived just a few houses down the street, over for dinner. While they were finishing dinner, the couple's cell phones started ringing and ringing. They just would not stop ringing!

The next day, Jessica found out that the nieces and nephews of this couple had been picked up by the Department of Human Services. The family was calling this couple to ask them to take these four children, so that they would not be put in just any foster home. The family wanted these four children to be able to remain together, and if placed in a foster home, the boys could be placed in a different home than the girls.

It is hard enough on the children to be taken away from their parents, but to be separated from each other would be even harder. The oldest boy had been the caregiver for his siblings, and the year old girl would not eat, after the separation. God knew the outcome long before it happened. It was no accident that this couple was with Jessica and her husband that night. The fact is that God often prepares people in advance for what is about to take place in their lives.

It was through this situation that Jessica came to meet these children, who would later become her own sons and daughters. The oldest was four, and the youngest was six months old. These children were very small for their ages and appeared to be malnourished. Jessica remembers thinking "I worked in DHS and Child Welfare all through college, but these were probably the most neglected children I have seen in a while". The oldest two even had rickets, which is a third world country issue. They could not talk and they were not potty trained.

The lack of development that was displayed by these children was very unsettling to Jessica, so she became involved. Every day after work, she would go down the street and spend time with them. Her husband worked the 2:00 to 10:00 shift, so she didn't have anybody waiting for her at home. She would go help with dinner, play with the kids and give them their baths — whatever needed to be done. She started watching the kids on weekends, so that the other couple could spend time with just their own two boys.

Jessica was beginning to build a relationship with these children which would go on for years to come. That is just what the Lord does with people. He builds a relationship which is to last a lifetime and beyond. He lets us know a little about Himself at a time, so as not to scare us, but to keep us interested. In fact, God compares our relationship with Him to a marriage, which is intended to last a lifetime. God courts people just like a man and a woman court each other, with the intention of spending a lifetime together.

Whenever the Department of Human Services (DHS) intervenes, their goal is reunification of the family, and that's the way it should be. But, this relationship was being built between Jessica and these children, by the grace of God. At the same time, these children were living with their aunt and uncle, so it was a very difficult time for their family. It would have been hard for this couple's own children to understand why, all of a sudden, they had four more children living with them, that were kind of like siblings, and took much of their mom's time.

It was a very trying time, so Jessica became their respite care, which is what it's called in the foster care world. She took care of these children almost every weekend. Then, to complicate things more, Shawn, the uncle with whom they were staying, who is a Marine, learned that he was about to be deployed. The children would need to be placed in another home, but where? There was the possibility of their maternal grandmother, and her husband, their step-grandfather, taking them. But, they lived next to the biological family. They saw all of the neglect, and never stepped in to help these children.

Jessica decided that now was the time to really fast and pray. Her husband, Russ, was about to leave on a hunting trip. But, he told her she should tell Shawn, the uncle, they would be willing to take the children, and she should go to the next court hearing. In the foster care world, you must have foster parenting classes, be fingerprinted, and have background checks. In fact, to take on children, you're supposed to be related by blood, or be an approved foster home. But again, Jessica fasted and prayed, then went with the aunt and uncle to court.

When the judge asked where they should be placed, Shawn gave Jessica and Russ's names. To Jessica's surprise, the judge said, "Ok, this is where they're going to go". At the same time, God spoke to her heart saying "Ok, Jessica, you're going to do this for Me". Russ was gone hunting, so Jessica was immediately immersed, for two weeks, into being a single parent of four very young children. She was rushed right into being a mom. She found herself loving every minute of it, but, at the same time, really struggling. When she would take the kids for visits with their parents, she could see that the parents were not making the progress that they needed, to have these kids return home.

What should have been an in and out case for DHS, just kept dragging on and on, with nothing changing. The parents had just plateaued; possibly it was a relief for them. It had to be overwhelming for the parents of these four small children. They didn't have the education to really have great jobs. Financially, it must have been a huge struggle. So, they just enjoyed time to visit, once a week.

Jessica began to wonder if she should minister to the parents, or protect the children. Here were the parents who did not know the Lord, personally, and yet they did not seem open to what she had to say. This could have been because of her relationship to the children. Then, the Lord spoke to her again, and said "I have placed these children in your hands; this is your ministry right now". So, Jessica stopped pushing so hard to tell them about Jesus, but she continued to show them the Love of Christ. Loving people where they are, is what the Lord calls His people to do. As believers in the Lord Jesus Christ, we must always love people, no matter what their sin might be. This is not always easy.

There she was, without her husband, and when she called him for support, he seemed to be disinterested. He wasn't on the phone with her more than two minutes. Basically, he said "Ok, well I'm really sorry to hear that, bye." She thought to herself that maybe he was just letting her go because of the circumstances, so she brushed it off. At Easter, when they were going to have the services for her grandmother, at home, in Sheridan, a strange thing happened. She didn't have to work that weekend. She asked Russ to take the weekend off, so they could spend time together, but he never got around to asking for the time off.

Satan was at work in the life of Russ, as Jessica was about to find out. This is something that happens, when a person does something for the Lord. Satan hates the Lord, and will do anything to destroy or harm those who follow the Lord. If a person thinks he is doing something for the Lord, and he does not feel opposition from Satan, he had better take another look at what he is doing. Satan will always oppose the things of God, and the best way to fight against him is through prayer.

The Lord always knows what is going on in the spiritual world. He will work to prepare us for the battle, if we will just submit to him. Jessica felt like something was about to happen, and the children needed protection that could come only from God. Then, in the presence of all her family, she had her pastor pray over each child, for there was a battle being raged for the souls of these children. Things were about to take a major change, in the lives of Jessica and her children.

About ten days later, at midnight on a Friday night, Russ came in and said, "Hey, I'm leaving you". He had been out with friends, so she said "Ok, what time are you going to be home? It's really late". Again he said, "I am leaving you". After the third time, Jessica came to the realization that their life together was over. As she stood there, the Holy Spirit just spoke to her heart and, out of her mouth came, "What's her name?" Russ responded, "Well, there are actually two women. One is just a friend, and one is more than that."

Again, the Holy Spirit spoke to her, and she heard herself asking, "Have you been into pornography?" Immediately, he became very angry and irate. Satan does not like to be found out, and will strike out when confronted. For the next three days, Jessica worked night and day trying to restore her marriage, but unfortunately, it was not to be. At one point, Jessica said out loud "Get behind me, Satan, in the name of Jesus"! She knew Russ was not in his right frame of mind; in fact, Russ acted like Dr. Jekyll and Mr. Hide, at times.

So, there was Jessica. Her husband had left her, and it seemed that her world was falling apart. She had only one option, and that was to place everything in the hands of the Lord. She knew that DHS policy would be to remove the children from her home. But, the Lord had said that they were her ministry for now, so she again cried out to the Lord. God is always true to His Word, and is moved by prayer. He speaks to the hearts of believers and non-believers alike, for He will always accomplish His will.

Jessica called her case worker, to explain the changes in her home and marriage. The worker drove up from Claremore, along with the secondary workers from Washington County, to see Jessica, with the intent of making a decision about the children. The Claremore worker, who was not required to attend this meeting, took time out of her personal schedule to attend. She said, "You're going to leave these children right here; as the primary worker, I want them left." And again, against all odds, the children were left in the care of Jessica. So Jessica said, "Ok Lord," dropping to her knees once again. Something some Christians miss is, thanking the Lord, when He moves in their lives, but not Jessica!

When a person thinks that everything is under control, there is always something else to deal with, and this was the case in Jessica's life. Russ had told her that it was ok with him if she started staying home with the children. So, Jessica resigned her job with Conoco Phillips. She had asked that April 30th be her last day with them, which meant that on May 1, she would stay home with the children. The trouble was that Russ left her in the middle of April. Here she was, allowed to keep the kids, but she was now unemployed.

Jessica's immediate response was to cry out to the Lord once more, saying "What do I do, Lord?

She began to seek new employment, and got a job as a bank teller, which was a large cut in pay, from what she had been making at Conoco Phillips. Although she was able to survive, she always felt she could do better. Her parents owned the home in which she was living, and they lowered the rent to help her out. Later, she would find other employment which would fit her skills better.

Down deep in her heart, Jessica sought the will of God in her life. When Jesus taught His disciples to pray, He said to pray to the Father that His will would be done on earth, as it is in heaven. So, this is what Jessica did: she told God, "I need to know Your Will." This may seem a bold step, but how can a person seek to do God's Will, without knowing what it is? On her knees, she prayed, "I am going to be like Gideon, and put out a fleece before You, because I don't know what else to do. If you want me to have these children, I need a handwritten letter, from someone I do not know, that says I am going to be their mother. I need You to terminate the rights of the biological parents, and make them mine, Lord. Otherwise, please provide a good family, who will take them, or let them go home. I cannot emotionally keep going on like this, with all these questions, and I don't want to damage, or hurt the children."

One day, in May, Jessica went to her mailbox, and pulled out a letter from someone she didn't know, in Wyoming. She turned to her mother, who was visiting, and said "Mom, do you know this lady?" Her mother said, "Yeah, actually I do! Nancy goes to my Bible study". She opened the letter, and immediately began to weep, because it started out with "I've been led by the Holy Spirit to write you". Jessica knew, the second she read it, that this was the answer to her fleece. This is what she had asked the Lord for, specifically!

In this letter, Nancy shared her own amazing testimony about the adoption of her son, her divorce, remarriage, and everything she had been through. Nancy felt led to tell Jessica to stand still, let God be God, and that Jessica would be the mother to these children.

At the court hearing, her lawyer stood up and said, "I file for termination of the parents' rights." The state of Oklahoma had implemented a law that, after fifteen months, if there had not been real changes, the termination would be filed. It was very obvious to everyone that the parents were not even trying to make the necessary changes in their lives, in order to keep their children. Maybe, to them, it was such a relief not to have to deal with the responsibilities of these young children. In Jessica's mind, it was like, check box number one! It was the first sign, on the handwritten promise, God had given her.

In September, a jury trial was scheduled to terminate parental rights. Jessica testified. On the second day, at about 7:00 pm, she got a phone call, indicating that the jury had announced, they had chosen to terminate the rights of the parents. Those in the know would say that it's easier to get the death penalty, at a jury trial, than it is to get termination of rights of the parents, because it is so final. It is a done deal, as if the children were never born to them. On the other hand, the parents had thirty days after that ruling to appeal, and if it went to appeals court, one is almost guaranteed another two years, fighting the system. Jessica was so overwhelmed and thankful that she prayed all day, and read scripture out loud. She knew, in her heart, this was going to happen, but just hearing the words made her heart jump for joy!

Now she faced the thirty day wait to see what the parents would do. During that time, Jessica learned the true meaning of "Be still, and know that I am God". (Psalms 46:10) Believers all over the world know these words from scripture, but very few have actually learned to put them into practice. Jessica was, back in God's school, learning to be an even better follower of the Lord. Jessica faced still another dilemma, when the grandparents became interested in having the children. She had two things working against her. The grandparents were blood relatives, and she was making only $10.00 per hour, which might make it appear that she would not be able to support these children.

Toward the end of September, Jessica was finally legally divorced. That morning, she went to the judge by herself, and signed the paperwork, finalizing everything. She was on her way to work, when she received a call from the daycare, that her youngest son was sick, and she needed to go and get him. As a bank teller, any sick time was just lost time, one doesn't get paid for it. Her children, for whatever reason, during this whole time, had been sick a lot. In fact, she took more time off, in the few months she worked at that bank, than she had in her entire career. Satan was trying to get her down, and for a short while, he was quite successful.

She drove to the daycare and, as she sat sobbing in her jeep, she cried out to the Lord once more, saying, "God what am I going to do? Please help me." God always hears the prayers of His children and, with Him, there is never a coincidence. The Hispanic pastor, Sam, from the church where her children were going to daycare, was dropping off his son. He knew Jessica, saw her crying, and came over to her window, asking, "Are you ok?" She responded, "Oh, yeah, just a tough morning. I'm just crying it out before I go in, but I'm ok." He dropped off his son, came back out and said to her "Are you sure you don't want to talk?" She responded by saying "Oh yeah, I'm just talking to God out here in my jeep."

Sam then asked her what she was doing for work. She told him she was looking for something, other than the bank teller job. Sam's wife worked at Oklahoma Wesleyan University, and knew of a position that had just opened up. Jessica was sure that she didn't have the requirements, but Sam insisted that she should apply. Jessica went home, put together her application, e-mailed it in, and didn't really think any more about it, until she was called in for an interview.

Two days before the court hearing, to determine who would be the adoptive placement, Jessica, or the grandparents, Jessica got a phone call from Oklahoma Wesleyan University with a job offer. She was able to take all that information to court with her — the offer of employment, stating the salary and benefits. She was ecstatic, as off to court she went! She met with her lawyer and was informed to be prepared; "Nothing's going to happen today," he claimed. "The judge is going to hear their lawyer and she is also going listen to us; but no decision will be made today. The judge is just going to let us tell what we feel is best for the children." As Jessica and her lawyer walked into the court room, the grandparent's lawyer stood up, but the judge told him sit down. She didn't even hear this lawyer out. She said, "You've had eighteen months, you have not been involved, and these children have now bonded to someone else. End of story. They belong to Jessica. That's it!"

Then, God worked another miracle through this judge. The judge looked at the case worker, and said, "How quickly can we get this adoption done?" Normally, after the parents don't file an appeal, it takes at least one year, to one and a half years, to process everything. But the judge said, "Now, I want this done by December; everything done by December. This adoption is going to be done in December." Jessica just sat shaking, because she couldn't believe what she was hearing. When they all walked out, she had to ask her lawyer what the judge said. Was the judge really saying this is going to be done by December? The lawyer responded, "Yes that is exactly what she said. I have never seen her do this. I don't know what more to tell you, except that this is amazing!"

When God Speaks, Even The Courts Listen

God worked out His plan for the ruling, which is totally amazing! He can, and will, accomplish His Will, in His own perfect timing. My God is great beyond belief, and yet He is interested in even the small things of our lives. When I was young, I thought that my father could do almost anything, but now **I KNOW that my God can do anything!** When He speaks, people are moved to do things His way, to follow the leading of the Lord. In my life, God has used both those who believe in Him and those who do not. I do not know where this judge stands with the Lord, but I do know that He used her to accomplish His Will, for these little ones. On December 15th, Jessica adopted all four of these children!

Before the children were adopted by Jessica, the Lord gave them new names. The Lord has changed the names of many people in Scripture. The apostle Paul was named Saul, Peter was Simon, and Abraham was Abram, to name just a few. One day, when Jessica was at work, months before she adopted these children, God gave her their names, which are Karsen Lee Welty, Jaslynn Nichole Welty, Ellissa Ann Welty, and Jaden Kyler Welty. The way their names are spelled gives them special meanings. Karsen is derived from several names, but if broken down, they all have the meaning of warrior, and Lee means shelter from the storm.

Jaslynn is a derived name from Jasmine, which is a flower. Nichole means freedom of the people. Ellissa means consecrated to God. Her middle name is Ann, and it means gracious one. Jaden means Jehovah has heard, and Kyler means handsome one. All these are very special names with very special meanings. I am sure He will see to it that they live up to their names.

I believe the Lord has special plans for these children and is already at work in their lives. For some reason, the Lord has chosen to work through people, and without a doubt in my mind, I am sure He will use these children in a mighty way. The hand of God plucked these children from their birth parents, and brought them to Jessica. He named them, and He will prosper them, for He is God. I cannot wait to see what the Lord will do with them!

They are already living up to the names that God has given them. Karsen is very loving and he is also a warrior. In fact, one day while Jessica's mom visited, Jessica had deleted a picture that she didn't like, from her mom's camera, and her mom, just jokingly, patted her on the bottom, and said, "You weren't supposed to do that." Karsen hadn't seen all of what had happened, but he saw Jessica's mom swat her. He ran across the living room, and even though it was just a tap, and was not painful at all, he put himself between them. He began to beat her thigh, saying, "Don't hurt my mama, don't hit her, don't do that." He is very protective of his siblings and Jessica. It is very surprising what that little six year old boy can do. If asked, at any given time, where his siblings are, he will name where they are, even if they're not in the same room. If he's at school, and they're at daycare, he can tell you where they are, and who they're with, at any time, because he just knows.

Jaslynn has a love for people that is not often seen in a small child. Anywhere she goes, she asks, "Do I know them? Can I go meet them? Can I tell them my name?" Sometimes, she has to be warned that strangers are not always good. She has learned to always ask Jessica before she makes contact. But when given permission, she is gone before a person can blink, saying "Hello, my name's Jaslynn." When she sees a child who is playing alone, she'll be the first one to go to that child, and begin to make a friend. That's something God's given her.

Ellissa is the silent one. She is very sweet, but if something is wrong, she'll be the first to stand up and say, "Oh no, we are not doing that. You need to stop that." And, sometimes it surprises people, because she's normally just so quiet. God gave Ellissa such a sweet, gentle spirit, but she is always ready to stand up, when something isn't right.

Sometimes, Jaden needs to be told to be easy and gentle with people. He's a little bit rougher than the others. But, he is emotionally sensitive to the people around him. If someone's crying, he'll be the first one to give a hug, or go see if they're ok, with no reservations.

A person can easily see that the Lord still does speak, and those who listen to His still, small voice, will be used to accomplish His will. In the same sense, a person must be careful to test the spirits that he or she listens to, for there are many spiritual beings speaking to our minds. Scripture says that "Satan himself masquerades as an angel of light" (2 Corinthians 11:14), and he will attempt to lead the believer astray. The test is, to lay what you hear over the Word of God, which is the Bible, and see if they agree. God will never tell a person to leave their spouse, because this goes against His Word. He will never tell a woman that it is ok to sleep with her boyfriend, or vice versa, because, again, this goes against His Word. These are just two examples of things the demonic forces have gotten believers to do over the years, so be careful of the voices you listen to.

As you can see again, God was not fair in Jessica's life, for if He was fair, then she would still be dealing with the court system. He would have left her to work it out for herself, or these children would still be stuck in a family that just did not want them. But God is more than fair, and He will, at times, step into a situation, working out His perfect way, in His perfect time. So, again, I believe I can say without a doubt, that God is not fair. He is more than fair!

Things to Ponder

1. Does God still speak to His creation? If so how has He spoken to you?
2. Is it true that "there are no coincidences, when a person walks with the Lord"?
3. "Satan will always oppose the things of God." What are some things that the believer can do to fight against Satan and his schemes?
4. Have you had times in your life where you have been back in God's school learning to wait on God?
5. "A person must be careful to test the spirits that he or she listens to, for there are many spiritual beings speaking to our minds." How do you "test the spirits"?

3

Plucked From the Fire

Throughout all of scripture, the Lord has done some mighty things in the lives of His children. He rescued Joseph from the hands of his brothers and sent him to Egypt, where he was sold as a slave to an Egyptian, and later thrown into prison for something he did not do. There must have been times when Joseph cried out to the Lord, "What are you doing? Why is this happening to me?" Yet, in everything recorded, Joseph was faithful to the Lord. Because of God's preparation, Joseph was in a position, years later, to save his family from certain starvation. It was God's plan, all along.

Later, we read that God saved Moses from death, as a child, so He could use him to rescue the children of Israel from slavery, at the hands of the Egyptians. Although it would be eighty years after Moses' birth, God already had His plan to use Moses, to rescue His people.

Still later, God rescued Samson from the hands of the Philistines several times. He gave Samson such mighty strength that Samson could not be bound. But notice, all this time, Samson was not living for God. He lived for himself, and disobeyed God's laws. As a Nazirite, Samson was to be set apart to the Lord from birth. His hair was not to be cut, he was not to drink any fermented drink, and he was not to touch any dead animal, or person. He broke all of these laws, and he even slept with a prostitute. Yet God rescued him and used him to defeat and kill many Philistines, because this was God's plan for him. God always has a plan, and sometimes He uses ordinary people to work out that plan. It may seem unfair, but remember God is not fair, He is more than fair.

In the first chapter, I wrote briefly about an event that took place in 1994. The following is a more detailed look at that incident, and the mighty hand of God.

It was before 2:00AM, on Sunday morning, March 27. I was awakened from a sound sleep, to find our house on fire. The truth of the matter is, that I woke up to voices in the hallway of our mobile home. The voices I heard were of two people that I knew very well; they were arguing. I later learned that my daughter, Jennifer, had also heard the same voices, but when she heard them, they were just talking. I got up and went to the door, threw it open and shouted, "What is going on here?" But, all I found was a fire in the hallway; no one was there. Sometimes God gives people a small glimpse of the spiritual world; and this was one of those times. I believe that I heard an angel and a demon arguing about what was going to happen to me and my family. I also believe that the Lord was well aware of what was going to happen to us, long before it happened, for He prepared the way in advance.

Three years earlier, we'd enjoyed having Norm, a young foreign exchange student from Germany, stay with us. Norm planned to visit again in the summer of 1994, but God had other plans. Norm called to see if he could come for Easter, instead. This was also the night when our school had its Prom. We were excited about seeing Norm again, so of course we agreed, and Norm arrived on that Friday evening. We really appreciated Norm's help, after the fire, as he played a major part in helping us cope in this time of trial.

The Lord also prepared other people to help us. One of these was Ray Orthman, who was on both the fire department, and the ambulance crew. The night of the fire, Ray, and his wife, Rose, were at the Firemen's Ball, in Custer, Montana, about twenty miles from Hysham, Montana. Sometime around 11:00PM, Rose had asked Ray if he wanted a drink, but Ray immediately turned it down. Most times, Ray would have gladly had a drink or two, but that night, he responded by saying, "No, something is not right tonight." Ray and Rose left the party early, returned to Hysham, and called it a night.

Just before 2:00 AM, Rose woke up to find Ray sitting on the edge of their bed, getting his clothes on. Rose asked her husband what was the matter. Again Ray responded, "Something is not right tonight." Rose rolled over. "If something happens, the beeper will sound." But Ray continued to get dressed. He was completely dressed when the fire call came in, so all he had to do was go to the fire hall, which was just across the street from their home.

Ray ran across the street to the fire hall, and opened the doors for the fire trucks, as soon as the fire call came in. Just as he was hitting the fire alarm, a call came in for the ambulance. Ray immediately went to the ambulance hall, which is about three blocks away from the fire hall. Ray jumped into the ambulance and headed towards our home, which was about two miles out of town.

Scripture says, in Deuteronomy 31:8, "The LORD Himself goes before you, and will be with you; He will never leave you, nor forsake you. Do not be afraid; do not be discouraged".

Believers can rely on this verse. We can know that whatever happens, it is exactly God's plan for us, at that exact time in our lives. God has indeed prepared the way, and the believer just has to follow Him. It sounds simple, but in reality it is very difficult, because people have a tendency to think that they can do it themselves, and do not need any help.

That night, when I woke up, our bedroom had a strange glow to it; I believe that there, in the room with us, was one of God's angels, sent to protect us. This bedroom was well lighted, but the attached bathroom was pitch-black. When I opened that door to the voices, and saw the fire, I shouted to wake my wife, Linda, "FIRE, FIRE!" She scrambled into her robe, as I opened the window next to the door, and helped her out. As I started to follow her, I felt a tremendous amount of heat on my back. Opening the window had caused a draft, and the hot air coming off the fire, was rushing out the window, right across my back.

Immediately, I knew that this was not the way for me to get out, so I went to another window, but it seemed to be stuck. I could not open it. I thought I was doomed, so I cried out, "What now?" and felt in my heart to try again. With a lot of effort, I pushed on the window and it came open, providing me a way out. I jumped through the window, landing with a big 'thud'. All this time, Linda stood outside the other window, wondering what was taking me so long. She looked back through the window, and saw the room was pitch-black inside. Then she heard me hit the ground. What a relief!

As I picked myself up off the ground, I looked at my watch, and it was 2:20 AM. I had told my son, Brian, to be home by 2:00, so I looked for his pickup, but it was not there. I was not sure, although I had a pretty good idea that he and Norm had not made it home yet. We teach our children to obey their parents, for that is what they should do. Yet, my heart was glad that he had not obeyed. If he had, I was sure that he and Norm would have been hurt, trying to save us.

That left only one person inside, and that was our daughter Jennifer. Linda rushed around the house, to see if she could get to Jennifer, and I followed. She found Jennifer, standing at her window, terrified, and screaming for help. Linda told her to push out the screen and jump out, which she did, landing on Linda. They both were a little bruised, but alive; and when I saw them coming around the corner of the house, I felt very relieved.

There we were, outside in the middle of the night, but the keys to our vehicles were still inside. Linda told me where her purse was, in the coat closet, so I opened the door and crawled back into the house, in search of her purse and the keys. The problem is that I misunderstood her, and thought that she said beside the closet. Therefore, since I could not find them, I came out empty-handed. "Now what do we do?" went through our minds. The only answer was to walk to get help.

Linda led the way, as we walked away from our burning home. Jennifer followed, and I brought up the rear. As we reached the county road, Linda took off running to the nearest neighbor's house, which was about one mile away. She was barefoot, running on a gravel road, yet when she was later examined by a doctor, he could not find any bruises on her feet. He was amazed that she did not have a mark on her feet, after running on that gravel road. In my mind's eye, I pictured two large angels, one on each side, lifting her up as she ran.

When Linda was at the halfway point, a car came along and gave her a ride. The first neighbor was not home, so they continued down the road to the next house. But before she made the call, someone else had called in the fire. Soon, another car came by, and Jennifer got in with them, but I did not feel right about getting in the backseat of that small car. So, there I stood on the side of the county road, in just my underwear; not very good attire for a Christian businessman.

It was also quite cool that night, around 40 degrees Fahrenheit, which was actually good for me, as it kept my burns from going deeper. As I stood there shivering, the deputy sheriff, Steve, came driving down the road, lights flashing and siren going. He stopped, and I got into his car, then he drove right back up to the house. This was something I did not want to do, as I had just gotten out of there. As the car came to a stop, Steve asked me if anyone was still in the house. I said, "I do not think so, but I do not know where my boys are."

Steve jumped out of the car, and ran into the house, exposing his lungs to some very toxic smoke. As Steve came out, one of the neighbor boys came over to the car, and told us that both Brian and Norm were still in town. What a relief! God had kept us all in His care. But this was just the beginning.

Soon, the ambulance arrived. The staff had me get out of the car, and lie face down on the stretcher. They lifted me, on the stretcher, over the trunk of the car, and into the ambulance. We headed for Billings, about 70 miles away, but as we sped down the highway, the crew called for the HELP helicopter.

About 30 miles down the road, we met the helicopter, at a rest area. It was closed at that time of the year, so we parked next to the gate, and the helicopter landed on the other side. The helicopter crew came into the ambulance and began to hook up IV's, and whatever else they needed. Then, they told me they were going to give me a shot to relax me, so they could put a tube down my throat, to keep my airways open.

Unfortunately, I relaxed a little too much, that is to say I quit breathing. So, the ambulance crew had to force air into my lungs, while trying to get that tube down my throat. After three attempts, the nurse could not get the tube down my throat, so the other technician took over, and placed it on his first try. All this time, the ambulance crew, including Ray, was concerned about my well-being. Ray said it did his heart good to see the color returning to my bald head.

They loaded me into the helicopter, in what seemed a tight compartment, and we headed for St. Vincent Hospital, in Billings. There, I was wheeled down the hallway to the emergency room, and the trauma team took over.

Shortly after we left Hysham, Linda and the kids were loaded into the other ambulance, and they also headed for Billings. When they arrived at the hospital, they were ushered into the room where I was, and my heart jumped for joy, to see with my own eyes, that they were alright! Someone might tell you something, but when you can observe it with your own eyes, you know for sure.

As I lay there, I learned that I might be headed to Salt Lake City, Utah, to the burn unit at the University Hospital. They are much better equipped to handle someone burned as badly as I was. Jennifer had smoke inhalation so they took her into another room and began to treat her. The next thing I knew, another flight crew was introduced, and I was told I had five minutes to say goodbye to my family, before I left for Salt Lake City.

Sometime, while I was being administered to, a tube had been placed down my nose, along with the one down my throat. How do you tell your family goodbye, when you have tubes down your nose and your throat? Linda told me there was room on the plane, and she could come along, if I wanted her to. I was unable to talk, so I just shook my head, 'no'. She wanted to confirm this, so she asked, "Do you want me to stay here?" To this I nodded, 'yes'. As I squeezed her hand, the crew told us it was time to go, and off I went again.

I was loaded onto another ambulance and we drove to the airport, just one mile away. There, we boarded a small airplane, the stretcher was secured, and we took off. As I lay there, all I had to do was listen to the flight attendants, as I could not talk. They might ask me how I was doing, or if I needed any more pain medication, which I never did, but mostly they talked among themselves. At one point, I heard the pilot say that we had a tail wind, and I wondered how that could be. This meant that the wind was blowing out of the northeast; yet when I left the house; it was blowing out of the southwest, just the opposite way. Once again, it was confirmed that God was in control; He was blowing us to Salt Lake City.

One hour later, we arrived in Salt Lake City. We were met by another ambulance, and I was taken to the University of Utah Hospital Emergency Room. When I left our burning home, I had only my under shorts on, and in the emergency room, the hospital staff cut them off. That night, our home was completely destroyed, including all of our furniture and clothing. This left us with nothing of our personal belongings, but soon God would start to replenish them, in His mighty way.

My first two days are just a blur, for the most part, but I do remember my nurse telling me that my family had been given a place to live, rent free. This put my mind at ease. I still praise the Lord for His goodness to me and my family. It wasn't until later that I learned the details. Ina Haines, one of the local ladies had asked Linda, on Sunday evening, if she would like to use a vacant house, rent free, that she and her husband had for sale. Linda said that she would like to, thinking she could use the sleeping bags and camping gear, we had in storage.

On Monday morning, Linda, accompanied by our pastor's wife, headed to Billings, to get some necessities. These included new eye glasses, the cost of which the Red Cross covered. After spending the day in Billings, they returned to Hysham, and went to the Haines house. As Linda walked through the back door, she noticed that the lights were on. This house was completely furnished; there was furniture in the rooms, dishes in the cupboards, and food in the refrigerator. She thought to herself that she must have misunderstood Ina, so she started to leave. She was very careful not to make any noise, so that she would not disturb whoever was living there.

At this point, she saw a note taped to the counter addressed to her. The note welcomed her and our family, to our new home! The community had come together to clean the house, and fill it with furniture from their own homes; some things would need to be returned later. The cupboards were stocked with all the utensils for preparing and serving our meals. The refrigerator and pantry were stocked with groceries, and were actually overflowing. There was so much meat given, that someone from the community went to the local Market, and rented a locker. To make it feel more like home, they had even hung pictures and clocks. Both the linen closet and medicine cabinet were well-stocked. There were even extra toothbrushes and toothpaste. As one friend put it, "We had everything, as if we had been living there. The only things missing were leftovers and garbage." Also, a fund was opened at the local bank, to help us with our bills, and many gave to that as well.

Throughout the Bible, we find times when the Lord provided what the people needed. He provided a ram for Abraham to sacrifice, manna for the people of Israel to eat, and a way through the Red Sea, to name just a few. This same God provided for our needs, by using the people of Hysham! When He provides, He uses whatever means He chooses. He uses both the believer, and the unbeliever alike, to accomplish His Will. The Israelites had different names for God. Each one told of the things that God would do. Here they called Him, Yahweh Jireh (Yireh) which means 'the Lord will provide'.

I had seen the Lord do this type of thing in my life before, but not on such a large scale. One time, in the past, He had provided for my family, a box of groceries, when I did not even know that we were about out of food. I had let a man store his camper trailer in my lumber yard, and in return, he had given me a box of groceries that would have spoiled, if he had left them in the camper. The fact was that the Lord was using this man to take care of a need in my family. So, when He used the community of Hysham, Montana, I easily recognized His hand in this.

God does not always act this way. At times, He uses our circumstances to test our faith in Him. We must never become upset when the Lord provides for someone else differently than He provides for us. We do not know the circumstances around that person, or the mind of God. There have also been times when the Lord has not provided what I thought I needed, for one reason or another. But in every circumstance, I know His way is perfect.

Soon, the prayers of people all over the country went up to Heaven for me and my family, and the Lord began to heal my body. On Tuesday, the hospital crew removed the tubes from my mouth and nose. Now, I was able to talk again, and I am sure there were those who wished they could put those tubes back in. The Lord was doing mighty things for me, and I would give Him credit for what He was doing in my life. Twice a day, I was taken to the lowboy, to scrub off my old, dead skin. On my first trip to the tub, the nurse told me to just 'slither on down' in the water. I did as she said, but then I sat right back up. The pain was tremendous!

If you have ever been sunburned, and got it wet, you might have an idea of how I felt. I had second and third degree burns over 26 percent of my body, starting at my right fingers, and going up my arm to my back. My entire back was burned, along with my left shoulder, and my left hand. With these types of burns, the skin is destroyed, leaving the nerve endings exposed. So take that sunburn, and multiply it several times and you have an idea of how I felt.

Even though I was given pain pills, before entering the tub, the pain was very bad at first. The second night that we went to the tub, my nurse said the hair on my back could cause infection, and she was about to shave my back. It felt like she was removing a layer of skin with each stroke of the razor. I had shaved my face many times, but I was not prepared for this, so needless to say, I got very upset that evening. I have never been one to hold back. In fact, I had a very bad temper, and that night, I said some things that I should not have.

The Lord allows a lot of things to come into our lives, to see how we will handle them, and this was one of those times. He set the example of forgiveness, and He expects His children to follow that example. Before long, I knew I must repent of my attitude, and apologize for my words and actions. This nurse was just doing what was best for me, at the time, just as the Lord does many times, in our lives. We do not like it at the time. We might even scream, and have a temper tantrum. But, if we look back, we can see that what happened was the best thing for us.

The people of the Lord were praying for me, and my body was healing much faster than expected. Each nurse was responsible for taking me to the tub, and scrubbing off the old, dead skin. As I began to heal, I tried to give the Lord the credit, for the changes that were being made in my body. At times, I felt that I was a side show at the circus, as other staff would come to see the healing that was taking place. Physiotherapists, nurses, and doctors all came to see the remarkable healing.

Once, I heard a comment, "Wow, look at all those new skin buds." I remember saying to myself that I had never thought of myself as a garden, but I know who the Gardener is. God is able to heal us today, just like He did when He walked on this earth. He provided new skin for me. God was working on me, and I was telling everyone I could all about it. At the time, this was a little out of character for me, as I usually kept my thoughts to myself. But, how could I keep quiet, when the Lord was at work in my life? We see in the Gospels, that whenever Jesus healed someone, that person always told others. So, that is what I did as well.

I remember one nurse, in particular; her name was Laurie. Early one day, she said to me, "There is something different about you." This would have been a perfect chance to share with Laurie, about a relationship with Jesus, but I let it slip by. Sometimes, we get so wrapped up in ourselves, and what is happening in our own lives, that we do not take the time to think about others. This was one of those times. But, if we are faithful to the Lord, He will provide another opportunity. Throughout the rest of that day, I shared with Laurie about what the Lord was doing, with me and my family. As her shift came to an end, I said to her, "I have been talking about my spiritual life all day long; how is yours?" Her reply was, "Up until now, not very good. But, I think it is about to change." It is my prayer to see Laurie in heaven one day, not because of anything I said or did, but because of what the Lord has done for all of us.

Each day, my wife, Linda, called to ask how I was doing. Sometimes, I reported that the doctors considered the possibility of a skin graft, here or there. Later on, people called her, or came into our store and inquired about me. She shared with them what I had told her, and they put me on their prayer chains. Heaven was flooded with the prayer requests of God's people, seeking the Lord, in regard to my specific needs. People all over the country prayed for me, and the Lord honored those requests, by healing my body. Each time a skin graft was considered, it was later ruled out. The power of earnest prayer is mighty! In the end, I did not have any skin grafts, just new skin.

Not only did God provide us a fully furnished home to live in, when we needed it, but He also arranged for Norm to come at a time when we needed him. God protected our son, Brian, and Norm, by keeping them away from the fire. God plucked Linda, Jennifer and me from the fire, and healed our bodies, in remarkable time.

On April 8th, just twelve days after I was burned, I was released from the hospital. My brother, James, traveled from his home in Duluth, Minnesota, to Salt Lake City, and escorted me back home. Six weeks later, on May 21, we moved into our new mobile home, in the same place that our other home had stood. We had gone full circle, from having a home, furniture and clothing, to having nothing; back to having a home, furniture and clothing, once again. I had gone from the excruciating pain of a severe burn, to having brand new skin.

We serve an awesome God, who provides for us, even though we do not deserve it. Again, I would have to say that God isn't fair, He is more than fair!

Things to Ponder

1. Does God really prepare things in advance, that is, before something happens in the life of a believer?
2. Have you ever been caught in attire that is not proper for a Christian or is there attire that is not proper for a Christian to wear?
3. Does the Lord really provide for the needs of a believer? Or is it just a coincidence when a believer's needs are met? How has God provided for you?
4. At one point "I knew I must repent of my attitude, and apologize for my words and actions." What kind of effect does the believer have when he or she apologizes for the words and actions that have been used?
5. Sometimes "we get so wrapped up in ourselves, and what is happening in our own lives, that we do not take the time to think about others." How can we change this?

4

Have Your Way, Lord!

There is an old hymn of the faith, in which we sing, "Have Thine Own Way, Lord!" When Jesus taught His disciples to pray, He said to pray, "Your will be done". (Matthew 6:10) This instruction is sometimes very hard to follow because we don't really want 'God's will'; what we really want is 'my will'. One of the hardest things to do is, to "let go and let God". There is a fear of letting go, for the question arises, "Will God really provide what I want?" Worse yet, "Will God allow something in my life that might be painful?" The question is really, "Can I trust God?" This is something that the believer must work at, and it does not come easily.

Let me illustrate that: When our children were young, we used to go to Trails End Ranch, in Ekalaka, MT. This is a Christian camp, in eastern Montana, mainly for young people, but they do have family retreats on holiday weekends. The camp has a lot of activities for the campers, including a zip line. A cable stretches between two hills, about one hundred yards long, with an apparatus to which one attaches a harness. When a person is all hooked up, he or she runs and jumps off the platform, riding the zip line across to the other hill, which is lower. I had watched my children do this many times, so I decided to give it a try.

I got all hooked up, ran and jumped, but I did not trust the harness. Maybe, I even forgot I had it on. So, what I did was to hold onto the rope, between the apparatus and the harness, all the way across the cable. My arms hurt, my muscles cried out in pain, and I wondered if I was even going to make it to the end. All I had to do was to sit down in the harness, and enjoy the ride, but I could not bring myself to do it!

That's the way it is, in our walk with the Lord. If we will just allow the Lord to have His Way, we will be in for a wonderful ride! But, first we must learn to truly trust the Lord. Trusting in the Lord is something that happens down deep in our hearts. Trust tells us, whatever He allows to happen in our lives, is what is best for us at the time. The following testimony is about a family who really trusted in God, and saw Him move in a mighty way.

Rex and Laura Welty live in Sheridan, Wyoming, and are the parents of Jessica Welty, (Chapter 2 When God Speaks, Even The Courts Listen). Rex experienced some numbness in his left arm, for an extended period of time, and was diagnosed with a ruptured disc, in his neck. For nearly two years, he woke up with headaches, and went to bed with headaches.

On Saturday, December 4, 2004, Rex again woke up with still another headache. It started just like every other day; but they would soon find out it was far from a normal day!

Laura, Rex's wife, planned to go to Billings with a friend, to do some Christmas shopping, which included buying Christmas gifts for some of Rex's employees. Laura asked him about getting a certain thing for one person, what she should look at, for this other person, and so forth. While she was talking to him, Rex complained about his headache and held his head. This whole time, he just gave her one syllable word answers. Then, she asked him, "How's your headache"?

He just kind of nodded, and she continued to chat away. It is easy to get so wrapped up in what we are doing that we do not know what is happening around us.

At this point, she realized that Rex was not answering. They were lying in bed, with Rex lying on his side. He was very calm, wasn't upset, and wasn't panicky. Again, she asked him "How's that headache?" He just smiled at her, and told her "yeah" a couple times. She responded by saying, "You need to answer me. I hate it when you don't answer me, when I talk to you!" Then she got up saying that she needed to call her friend to explain that she would be a little late. With the phone call done, she looked in the bedroom. Rex was still lying in bed, and was licking his lips.

She went into the bathroom, got a cup of water, and brought it over to him. He rolled from his side onto his back, with his legs spread out. She told him to put his legs together, and sit up, but he totally ignored her. She came to the side of the bed, took his hand to help him sit up, but he did not respond. Then, she put her arms around his shoulders, and got him in the sitting position. He calmly took the glass of water from her and started to drink it. Half of it spilled down his chest, but she still didn't put two and two together. One side of his mouth wasn't holding it in.

Have Your Way, Lord!

She gently laid him back down, and was still talking away at him. She was telling him, he really needed to talk to her, and to answer her. About a minute went by, when he turned, got up on his elbow and started to vomit. He only had about half a glass of water in his stomach, and she knew he should not be vomiting, with just water. She realized that something was wrong, and headed for the phone. But instead of calling the hospital, Laura called Rex's mother, Marion.

His mother is a registered dietitian, who had worked at the VA for a long time. She is very familiar with geriatric illnesses. Laura asked her, "Marion, what are the signs of a stroke? I can't remember what they are." Marion responded with, "What's going on?" Laura said, "Well, Rex won't answer me, and one side of his mouth isn't working". Marion immediately told her, "You call 911!" Laura, still unsure, said, "Okay, you think I should?" The answer came back, "Yes!" Laura then asked her, "Will you meet us there?" Marion responded, "We'll be right there!"

Laura was still in her nightgown, as she called 911. She told them, she thought her husband might have just had a stroke. She stated their address and explained that their bedroom was in the basement, so the ambulance crew would know to bring whatever it would take, to get Rex out of the house. The 911 operator kept talking to her. Laura felt she needed get dressed and call her prayer partner. She struggled to get this lady off the phone, but the 911 operators are required to keep callers on the phone, until someone arrives at the door. So, there she was, trying to get dressed with one hand, and hold onto the phone with the other. Half dressed, she ran upstairs, to unlock the front door, and then ran back downstairs, while the operator talked to the ambulance crew. So, as soon as she heard them rattle the front door, she said, "Ok they're here now. Bye".

Laura zipped her pants up, threw her shirt on, and quickly dialed her prayer partner. Sandy is one of those people Laura can call, day or night, no matter what's happened. They have prayed with each other for many years. But that morning, Sandy was in Casper, for a continuing education class, and instead, Sandy's husband, John, who is good friends with Rex, answered the phone. Laura explained that they were taking Rex to the emergency room, because he may have had a stroke.

All this time, Laura could hear the clomp, clomp, clomp, and step, step, step, step of feet, and knew that she had to be fast. She had to get John off the phone, as fear began to grip her. When John hung up, he called their Church secretary, who immediately got it on the prayer chain. They have a good chain of communication, at Rex and Laura's church, so within minutes; God was being bombarded with prayers, for both Rex and Laura.

Rex and Laura had been teaching a young adult Sunday school class, in which they had two firemen/ EMTs. Laura was hoping one of them would be there, but neither one of them came. The EMTs came in and looked at Rex. He was awake, but wasn't talking to them. He appeared to be in slow motion, when he did move, but he couldn't move very much.

Laura was told that Rex had probably had a stroke. He was moved onto a stair chair, and taken out of the basement. There, they had a regular gurney which took him to the ambulance. Later, Laura found out that one EMT had said, "He's dead, and just doesn't know it". People can, and do, have their opinions, but God is God, and He alone will determine the outcome. That thought should not have been expressed. This situation may not seem fair, but remember God is not fair.

On her way to the hospital, a verse from scripture came to Laura's mind: "See, I have engraved you on the palms of My hands" (Isaiah 49:16). Engraving is not just a flat surface, like a tattoo, but is a carving into the surface. God is saying, "You are right here, in My palm, you are part of Me".

Laura met her in-laws, just outside of the hospital. As the three of them held hands to pray, another scripture came to her mind: "Give thanks in all circumstances, for this is God's will for you, in Christ Jesus" (1 Thessalonians 5:18). So they prayed that verse, knowing that Rex is engraved in God's Hand. Out of obedience, they were giving thanks, in faith believing for a good outcome, even though it didn't seem very positive at the moment.

Then, they went into the Emergency Room. Both of their pastors were out of town that day, but God's people began to gather at the hospital waiting room. A rancher cleaned up and came. A paralyzed man, in a wheel chair, was at the construction site of a new home that was being built for him. He was there without his special van, so four guys picked his chair up, put it in the back of their pickup, and drove him down to the emergency room. As they gathered, they began to lift up Rex and Laura before the Lord.

The doctors required a CT scan, to determine if it was a bleed, or if it was a clot that caused the stroke. If it was a clot, they could use a clot buster drug, but if it was a bleed, this could not be used.

They took Rex in for the CT scans, and the first batch was really bad, because he kept vomiting. Even though the image was very fuzzy, they could tell that it was a bleed because it was so huge; it was not a clot. This ruled out the clot buster drug, because this would cause him to bleed even more. There are two types of strokes; they are thrombotic stroke and hemorrhagic stroke. Thrombotic stroke is caused by a blood clot and a hemorrhagic stroke is caused by a hemorrhage, or bleed.

In her mind, Laura could hear her daughter, Anna's, little voice saying, "Mom, if you or Dad ever have serious health concerns, go to Billings. Do not stay in Sheridan, go to Billings." Anna was studying to be a nurse. In a short time, the doctors said to Laura, "You probably need to take him to Billings". She responded, "Yes, we will go to Billings". They informed her that she could go with Rex, so she went home to pack a few things. While she was gone, all the people in the waiting room gathered around Rex, anointed him with oil, and prayed for him. Usually, they let only two people at a time visit a patient, in an emergency room. But these were not usual circumstances, so all 14 or 15 people lifted Rex, and the family, before the Lord.

While all this is happening, Rex's mother began to call his daughters in Oklahoma. Jessica's reaction was one of doubt. After all, Rex was only 47; he was much too young to have a stroke. Marion was not able to reach Anna, so she asked Jessica to tell her. Anna and Jessica were students at Oklahoma Wesleyan and, if you have to be in a crisis, a Christian campus is a great place to be. They were immediately surrounded by God's love for them, through His people.

As Laura arrived back at the emergency room, Tony, who was in the wheel chair, handed her his cell phone and said "Laura, if you're going to Billings, you're going to need this. I know you don't have a cell phone." Jessica had that number, called in, and said, "I want to talk to my dad". Laura held the phone up to his ear, and as Jessica spoke, Rex sobbed. They were loaded in an ambulance, driven across town to the airport, and then flown by helicopter, from Sheridan to the top of St. Vincent Hospital. They had intubated him, and put him in an induced coma, so he would be still and calm during that time.

Just as they arrived at Billings, Rex began to come out of the coma and started to remove his tube. The Emergency Room staff had trouble reinserting the tube, so the nurse from the helicopter came in and did it. During this time, Laura was asked to leave the emergency room, so she used the time to call Harvey Bybee, a retired Wesleyan minister. Harvey now owned a bed and breakfast, in Billings. Laura had worked with him at teen camp, when He was still pastoring a church. Laura asked Harvey, "Will you come to the hospital and be my pastor"? He was there in a short time.

It was time for the Winter Banquet at Oklahoma Wesleyan University. Anna and Jessica were planning to go, and it was Anna's first real date. Neither one of them wanted to go, but they had promised their dates that they would, so they went. About half way through the banquet, Dr. Piper (president of the University) tapped Jessica on the shoulder, called her out into the hall, and asked, "Have you made arrangements to take your finals next week"? She replied "No, my mom suggested that we try to take them all on Monday, and then fly out". He said, "You know, I think you probably should go home, and the school will pay for half of your airfare home". Oklahoma Wesleyan University paid for one ticket.

During the previous two summers, Jessica had worked as a nanny for a movie director in Dayton, Wyoming. Jessica had texted his wife, Kate, saying, "Please pray for my dad". Kate knew of the situation, so she replied "Your mom is telling you not to come home for a few days. I'm telling you, you need to get home!" Kate got on the Internet, bought a ticket for each of the girls, and paid for them with her credit card. The school reimbursed her for one of the tickets. The

Lord uses people to accomplish His will, and we can see that many were being used, as He responded to the prayers of His faithful servants.

Laura met with the neurosurgeon, who told her the biggest danger, after a stroke, is swelling on the brain. The skull does not expand, so sometimes he has to take out a four inch piece of skullcap, freeze it, and reinstall it later. This allows the brain to expand. Then they go in and suction out the blood. He also told her that he hates to do that surgery because, every time he does, it causes permanent brain damage.

They had put in what they called a bolt, by drilling a little hole through the skull and inserting a devise between the two hemispheres of the brain, which then drains off bloody spinal column fluid. This allows them to tell what the pressure inside the brain is. They put Rex on a monitor, wanting that monitor to stay under 20. The biggest danger of swelling is usually between 48 and 72 hours. Laura needed to know this, so she would be ready to make a decision, when and if the pressure got too high.

Jessica and Anna flew in the next day, so they were all together, as they waited to see the outcome. Rex owned his business. He did a lot of public speaking, including making the announcements every Sunday, in church. Now, Rex was silent, and in a bed, with tubes running everywhere. One at a time, the girls went in see their dad, and try to make sense of the situation.

The next Sunday night, Laura and her daughters stayed at Harvey Bybee's bed and breakfast, The Josephine. About 1:00 AM, the phone rang. Laura answered. It was the neurosurgeon and he had some very difficult news. "Okay, Laura, the time has come. Rex's intracranial pressure is up in the 40s, and we've done everything we can medically, to bring it down. The time has come for you to make the decision about taking out a piece of skull and letting his brain expand, to relieve the pressure." Laura was a mess! As she spoke to the doctor, she relayed his message to her girls who sat right beside her.

Jessica said, "Mom, I know just what Dad would want. He would either want to go home to be with Jesus, or he would want every chance he could have, to be whole. Do not allow the doctor to take out that piece of skull." Laura agreed, and relayed their decision to the doctor that they did not want to have the surgery.

He responded "Well, I need to tell you that he probably will not live through the night". Laura said, "I understand. We're going to put him in God's hands."

God Is Not Fair, He Is More Than Fair

In the Old Testament, God told Abraham to put his son on the altar, and sacrifice Him to the Lord. This was a test, to see if Abraham really trusted God with Isaac. The Lord often asks us to trust Him, and let Him have His Way, but all too often, we hold on, and miss out on seeing Him do a mighty work, in our life. So Laura prayed "God, Thy will be done. Whatever You see is the best, You do it, because I don't even know what I think is best." Laura put Rex on the altar, and left it up to the Lord.

Abraham had passed the test, and so did Laura and the girls. God does not test us so He will know how we will react. He already knows what we will say and do, for He is all-knowing. He allows us to be tested, so that others will see that our faith in Him is real. People are watching to see if this faith we claim is real, or if, when the going gets rough, we will give up.

About 25 minutes later, the phone rang again. The neurosurgeon called with good news, this time. "Well, Laura you made the right decision. We don't understand it, but his intracranial pressure has gone down to 16, and stabilized. The way things usually go, the intracranial pressure usually goes up, up, up, evens out, and they die. Usually, it's 20 minutes. We really were not expecting this." Somewhere in that

25 to 30 minutes, God did the first miracle for Rex! Even the neurosurgeon had to admit, this was a miracle.

Laura and the girls stayed at The Josephine, in a two bedroom suite that Harvey usually charged $100 per night for, but he let them stay for only $200 per week. God then opened up the flood gates of heaven. People just walked up and handed her 50 and 100 dollar bills. During that time, they received over $6000 from friends, family, Church family, and customers. Rex's customers, who had supported his business for years, gave them more money. Each one had his own reason, but one gift stood out with this comment: "One time Rex checked out my van for free, and I really appreciated it. He said that I didn't owe him anything; he'd catch it next time. I know you can use this." Every day, cards enclosing gifts of money arrived and these funds covered every cost of their stay. One woman from their church offered to pay for their suite for a week. Someone else offered to cover another weeks' stay. God truly was looking after their every need.

But one day, Sandy, Laura's prayer partner, asked Laura, "Doesn't this bother you? I mean, you guys have been great volunteers in the church, and you both work with youth. You've worked in finances, and Rex was the treasurer of the church. How could God let this happen to somebody who's faithfully working for Him? How could He allow this to happen?"

Laura's response clearly showed Sandy her faith in God's word. "Remember the story of Lazarus? He was sick and his sister, Martha sent word to Jesus. But Jesus waited three more days, before He came to their home." She continued, "Jesus explained that this sickness was not unto death, but it was so the Lord would be glorified. I know that what has happened to Rex is also going to bring glory to God!"

Later, Sandy ran into Dan, Rex's employee, who ran the shop, while Rex was in the hospital. She said to him "Boy, it really bothers me that this happened to Rex!" Dan responded, "You wouldn't believe the people that come into the shop, and we're talking to them about spiritual things — all because Rex had a stroke." God had given them an open door, to tell people of His love.

Rex spent 18 days, in the Intensive Care Unit (ICU), on a ventilator. Once the machine was breathing for him, they really had to work to get his lungs going again. He could not leave the ICU, until he was breathing on his own, and his oxygen saturation levels were right. But when that happened, he was moved to the 5th floor, which was the Intermediate

Care Unit. This floor had many patients with stroke, brain, and spinal column injuries.

The family had a very memorable Christmas, in the hospital. They brought in a tree and completely decorated it for Rex's room. The night before his stroke, Rex had wrapped his gift for Laura — an anniversary band, with ten tiny diamonds. In an effort to conceal his gift, Rex wrapped it in a big box, with extra things to increase the weight. After Rex had his speaking valve inserted, Jessica came to his room, and played 50 questions with him. He was still struggling to speak. She asked about Laura's gift so that she could bring it to the hospital. "How big is the box?" Rex could move only one hand, so he had difficulty explaining the size. He responded, "It's a large box," but Jessica thought he said "lock box". She asked about the color, and he told her it was green. Jessica tore the storage room apart searching for a green lock box, but didn't find one. At last, she found the correct box and Laura received her ring!

Rex was moved once more on December 26, and started rehabilitation the next day. He began in a wheelchair, with three hours of treatment each day. He had to learn to do almost everything all over again. After three weeks in Rehabilitation, he was told to expect another six weeks of treatment. But, in half that time, he was walking, climbing stairs and maintaining his balance.

One morning, the therapist had Rex working to try to lift his foot, and slide his heel forward, in order to walk. He couldn't do it that morning, but by that afternoon he could. He made progress by leaps and bounds — phenomenal progress! The staff interviewed Rex and Laura, before they could go home; they wanted to be sure that the house was suitable. The master bedroom was in the basement, which normally would have been a problem, because of the stairs. But, Rex had been going up and down stairs at the hospital. The only change necessary was hand rail on both sides of the stairs, so that Rex's strong hand would have a rail, whether he was going up or downstairs.

When Rex no longer needed a cane or walker, they checked out and went home. His physical therapist commented, "I've been doing this for ten years; I have never seen a patient progress so quickly, in such a short period of time."

Four and a half months after his stroke, Rex developed seizures. Laura woke up to find the bed shaking; Rex was having his first seizure. This happens to 14 percent of people who have strokes. In fact, it is more common for people who

Have Your Way, Lord!

have a hemorrhagic stroke, to develop seizures. His lips were blue, and Laura thought he was dying. For Laura, this was more frightening than the actual stroke. The seizure lasted several minutes. This time, Laura called 911 immediately, but by the time the emergency people arrived, the seizure was over, and Rex had dropped into a deep sleep.

The ambulance crew took Rex to the hospital, where he was examined. The nurse in the ER was the same nurse who attended Rex when he had his stroke. They kept him for two hours, did another CT scan, and released him, because they could not find anything wrong. The nurse watched Rex dress himself, as he was getting ready to go home. She stood, amazed. All the nurse could do, was stand there and shake his head, saying, "Unbelievable, unbelievable!" People are always amazed, when the Lord does a miracle, and Rex is definitely a miracle. In time, the seizures stopped, and Rex appears to be as normal as anyone.

As I interviewed Rex and Laura, I could see that they are very humble people. They praise the Lord for all that He did, and continues to do, in their lives. God is not fair. He works miracles, without regard to whether a person deserves it, or not. Again, let me say, "God is not fair, He is more than fair!"

Things to Ponder

1. Do we really want God's will to be done or do we want my will to be done by God?
2. Is it important to "Give thanks in all circumstances"? Or is it only important to thank God when He does something that we "like"?
3. People provided a way for Rex's daughters to fly back to be with him. Is this something that the believer should do for his/her fellow believers only or should the believer be willing to do this for anyone, even someone who is living in sin?
4. Abraham was willing to put his son on the altar, and sacrifice Him to the Lord. Is there anything you are not willing to give up for the Lord?
5. When Rex developed seizures, it could have been the beginning of a time of doubt for Rex and Laura. Are there times when the believer doubts what God does and if so, how could he/she combat those times?

5

It's All Worth It

As I was growing up, when I did something stupid, and had gotten hurt, my parents would ask me, "Well, was it worth it?" Most of the time, I would answer, "yes!", even though I knew in my heart, it was not. I loved to ride motorcycles, and sometimes I would tip one over, and would come home all scraped up. But, I would never admit that I had done anything wrong, and would usually blame someone else, for what had happened to me.

Now that I am older, I have found I can always say, "It's all worth it". That is, when I'm following the Lord! But, sometimes I have to admit that I do question it. There are, and will be, times that every believer cries out to God, when things seem to keep going wrong.

Scripture says, in Romans 8:28, "we know that, in all things, God works for the good of those who love Him".

Although most believers know this verse, we have a tendency to forget it, when the going gets rough. It's like the old saying that goes, "It's hard to remember, when you're up to your knees in alligators, that your objective is, to drain the swamp!" The problem is, we cannot see the end results, so we focus on the things happening around us. Instead, we should rely on the Lord, and not on our own strength. That sounds easy, but it is actually very difficult. With this thought in mind, let me tell you about what happened to my family, in August of 1994.

On a Saturday, in August, my wife, Linda, and I were sitting in the waiting room, of Deaconess Hospital, in Billings Montana. Our daughter, Jennifer, was having brain surgery, at the time, and we were very concerned for her. Her shunt had become plugged, so she had to have emergency surgery.

To really understand, we must go back to January 30, 1980, when Jennifer was born. We had just recently moved from Billings, Montana to Hysham, Montana, a distance of about seventy-five miles. Early that morning, Linda woke me, to say it was time. We quickly got dressed, and headed to the hospital in Billings, for the birth of our second child. Jennifer was born that morning, but there was a problem.

Jennifer was jaundiced. She would need to be taken every day to the hospital, for a bilirubin test. I had to return to Hysham, to take care of the hardware store we had just purchased. So, Linda, our son, Brian, and the baby, stayed with my parents, in Billings, and my mother took them to the hospital each day, for Jennifer's test.

One morning, as Linda was getting ready to take Jennifer to the hospital for her test, she noticed that Jennifer felt warm to her. She took her temperature, and found it to be a little above 98.6 Fahrenheit. So she talked to the nurse doing the bilirubin test, and asked her what the normal temperature for a baby was. In the course of the conversation, the nurse advised Linda that Jennifer should be seen by a doctor. They were referred to a pediatrician, who examined Jennifer, and ordered a spinal tap.

The spinal tap revealed that she had old blood in her spinal fluid, which indicated that Jennifer had had a bleed in her head, at some point, before, during, or after birth. She was immediately placed in the pediatric ICU, and monitored. Her head was measured daily. It was growing in diameter, indicating a block, probably from a blood clot, in the ventricle, where her spinal fluid drained from her brain.

When Jennifer was eleven days old, a wonderful Christian neurosurgeon drilled a hole through our baby girl's head, into her brain, and installed a shunt to drain off spinal fluid. A shunt is a little tube that goes into the brain. A valve, under the skin on the head, collects the fluid, and a tube runs under the skin, from the valve to the abdomen, where the fluid drains and is absorbed.

The surgery took five hours. As I sat with my wife, Linda, in the waiting room, the peace of God came over us. We had put Jennifer into His hands, had given Him complete control over the situation, and were willing to accept whatever the outcome would be. We had a peace I had never experienced before, but have several times since.

In Scripture, we read, from Phil 4:6-7 "Do not be anxious about anything, but in everything, by prayer and petition, with thanksgiving, present your requests to God. And the peace of God, which transcends all understanding, will guard your hearts and your minds in Christ Jesus".

Over most major things in our lives, we have no control. We can either be afraid of the outcome, or accept the fact that, whatever God allows in our lives, is what is right, at that time.

If we allow the Lord to be in control, He will do some mighty works. But all may not be what we would like Him to do, and some may even be painful to us. In all things, we can have "the peace of God, which transcends all understanding".

After the surgery, Jennifer was closely monitored, and her head measured daily. Her head continued to grow. Something was wrong, and the neurosurgeon determined, that the first valve he had put in Jennifer, was defective. So, back to surgery she went, this time to replace the defective valve. Our faith was tested again. This time, the valve worked, and her head began to return to normal, but our ordeal was far from over.

Linda called Pastor Jim, at our church, asking for prayer, and he brought his wife, Rosemary, up for a visit. The Lord had compelled her to come and share, with Linda, the experience they had with their son. He had been seriously ill, and the doctors had given up on him. They told Rosemary and Jim there was no hope for their son. Instead, they should make arrangements to put him into a special home. Pastor Jim and Rosemary chose to take their son home, and to raise him themselves. Well, God saw fit to completely heal their son. Rosemary shared, that sometimes, they had a hard time keeping up with him.

Linda had to take Jennifer for numerous checkups with the neurosurgeon. He was very good at explaining everything — what tests he was doing and what he was looking for. He was also honest enough to tell her, that most children with shunts have problems with them often, such as blockages and infections. This very capable doctor also explained that as a result of Jennifer's bleed and surgeries, there was a chance that she could be retarded, slow, handicapped, and perhaps even unable to walk.

Before Jennifer was born, we had watched the 'Roots' series on TV. In one scene of this movie, the father of Kunta Kinte is shown, lifting his baby up in his hands, to his God. Linda often pictured herself lifting our daughter up to God, and giving her to Him. We also prayed, telling God that whatever He wanted, we would do our best to deal with it. If He chose for her to be retarded, or unable to walk, or handicapped, we would accept it.

The Lord was definitely in control throughout this situation; He provided us with the right pediatrician. He blessed us with a Christian neurosurgeon. I wouldn't be surprised to find out that he prayed over our daughter's surgeries, and about the defective valve. We were sad when he retired, and frustrated with the neurologists, we had to deal with afterward.

Shunts last but a few years, and it is normal to have them become plugged often, or become infected. They also must be replaced often. God chose to let Jennifer grow up to be normal. Thankfully, she was not retarded or handicapped, but was just a normal little girl. Also, her shunt lasted for an abnormally long time.

Over the next fourteen years, Jennifer had bouts with migraine headaches. Many times, we took her to neurologists, and they would send her through a CT scan, and tell us it was not her shunt. The CT scan would show that everything was normal. But, what I have found over the years is, that there is no normal, there is average. God has made each and every one of us different, in certain ways.

Then, 14 years after she was born, in August of 1994, things took a major turn in our lives. She and Brian, our son, were headed to a church camp, south of Gillette, Wyoming. They had gone to Forsyth, the night before, and stayed with our pastor's family. That night, Jennifer had a horrendous headache, but she thought it was just another one of her migraines. When she woke up the next morning, and opened her eyes, it appeared as if she was looking through a water bubble, in some spots.

They went to the church, but afterward, when they started off for the camp, Jennifer was sick to her stomach. They all thought it was just a bug, or an upset tummy, so they tried using Pepto-Bismol to settle her stomach. In the long run, nothing worked, and she was sick all the way to camp. Every so often, they stopped the van so she could get out and vomit. When they arrived at the camp, Jennifer went straight to her bed, and stayed there.

For the next few days, Jennifer did not go to the dining hall, or to any of the activities, but remained in her cabin. Her counselor became very concerned about her, and reported this concern to her leader. They talked to Jennifer about returning home, but each time, she asked to stay. Finally, all the counselors gathered around Jennifer, and prayed for her.

The next morning, our Pastor, Harvey Bybee, told Jennifer she needed to return home, and this time she was ready to go. Harvey called me, and told me the situation. He had arranged for one of the youth pastors to bring Jennifer as far as Biddle, Montana. Biddle is a very small town (population 8), in southeastern Montana. It is the halfway point between Hysham and the camp.

I headed for Biddle in my pickup truck, the only thing on my mind, was getting there and back, in as short a time as possible. We needed to get Jennifer to a doctor, as quickly as we could. When I arrived, I could quickly tell that Jennifer had not yet arrived. For the next two hours, I sat there with nothing to do, other than to become angry. I have found that God's timing is perfect, and ours is not. I had just experienced a prime example of this, and I should not have become angry. But I am human, so I fail every so often.

Finally, they arrived! After Jennifer was settled in the pickup, we headed for home. She didn't say much, just drifted off to sleep. Then suddenly, she started shaking all over. I spoke to her, and she did not answer. I spoke a little louder and still nothing. Then, I starting yelling at her, and there was still no response. All kinds of thoughts started flowing through my head, and I had no idea what to do. She was having a seizure, and I had never experienced anything like this before. Was I losing my daughter? I didn't know. The only thing I could do was to pray, and pray I did!

As time passed, I drove and prayed. Then, after what seemed like about five minutes, the seizure was over. She had at least two more seizures, before we arrived back home. The next day, we began to visit doctors. We had taken Jennifer many times to see neurologists because of her bouts with migraine headaches, and all the doctors would do was send her through a CT scan, tell us that it was not her shunt, and send us home.

This time, we decided to try a different route. We visited a pediatrician who was very thorough. She ordered several tests, which all came back normal. Jennifer was going downhill, having seizures and going blind; so much so, that we had to lead her around. She slept more and more and ate less and less. As a last resort, the doctor decided to test her brain waves.

The test came back slightly irregular, so the doctor recommended that we take Jennifer to Emergency, in Billings. There we would see the Dr. who was on call. But when Linda and Jennifer arrived at the emergency room, this Dr. said, "You don't want to see me, I do surgery. You want to see the neurologist." After a short wait, Jennifer was able to see the associate, and guess what he did? Yes, he sent Jennifer through a CT scan! He also did some neurological tests on her, and even looked into the back of her eyes.

Linda knew that one should be able to see certain colors, in the back of the eye, and be able to tell if there is pressure on the brain, or not. She learned this from the neurosurgeon who put in Jennifer's original shunt, when she was 11 days old. However, this neurologist could not see anything. Linda questioned him about it and he said he didn't see anything back there. Then, he got frustrated with her, slapped the CT scan up on the screen, and showed her that it was normal. She asked him why Jennifer was practically blind, and was having seizures. He responded, "I don't know. Maybe she has some strange virus or something." Linda and Jennifer returned home, very frustrated!

One or two days later, Linda made another trip to Billings, to run errands for the hardware store. Jennifer was home by herself, when the phone rang. The neurosurgeon had his nurse call, to see how Jennifer was doing. Doctors don't typically check up on patients they haven't seen before. Could it have been the voice of the Lord, prompting him to do this? God still speaks in that still, small voice, to the hearts of people. The nurse asked Jennifer how she was doing, and she responded, "Everything's the same, pretty much".

After the nurse hung up, Jennifer decided to try and pump her shunt, and she felt a lot of pain, as the tube had gotten all kinked up. Since she didn't have a number for the doctor's office, she called me at the hardware store, by feeling the numbers on the phone. She told me about the call from the doctor's office, and that her shunt was plugged. I called the doctor's office, and was told to get Jennifer up there immediately!

I then called Linda, and told her to meet our son, Brian, and Jennifer, half way between Hysham and Billings. Linda and Brian traded vehicles, with Linda taking Jennifer to the doctor's office, and Brian bringing the loaded pickup back to the store. When Jennifer arrived at the doctor's office, he looked into the back of her eyes. He then called for an eye doctor to give his opinion.

The eye doctor looked into the back of Jennifer's eyes, and confirmed what the neurosurgeon found. The pressure was high! Jennifer needed to have her shunt replaced, right away. He apologized greatly, because he was scheduled for back-to-back surgeries, all the next day, but he could do the surgery the following day if Jennifer were at the hospital, by 6:00 AM. Linda asked him if Jennifer would get her eyesight back, after her shunt was replaced. He shook his head, no, and said there was no guarantee.

We arrived promptly at 6:00 AM. When all the paper work was complete, Jennifer was prepped for surgery. Years earlier, Linda had told Jennifer that her hair was almost black, when she was born, and after they shaved it off, to put in her first shunt, it grew in a different color. This time, in preparing for surgery, the medical staff wanted to shave only half of her head. She told them to shave it all off, because she was not going to have her hair, half one color, and half another.

After the surgery, the neurosurgeon reported to Linda and me, what he did, and how things went. He also told us that when Jennifer started feeling better, he would send her through a CT scan, to see if what he was thinking, was correct. He thought we would see that Jennifer had slit ventricles, so when they looked normal on a CT scan, it was not normal, for her. We went to see Jennifer, in recovery, and found her watching TV, reading everything going across the screen, and enjoying all the different colors! God had chosen to restore Jennifer's eyesight.

As followers of Jesus, we believe that all things will work together for our good. When it doesn't seem to be working out that way, we get angry with the Lord. But, He is always right there with us, as we pass through those difficult times. If He had not restored Jennifer's eyesight, He would still be God, and would be worthy of our praise.

When Jennifer went in for her post-surgery checkup and CT scan, the neurosurgeon showed us Jennifer's CT scans, from before and after surgery. It was very obvious that she does, in fact, have slit ventricles. We could really see the difference.

When school started, Jennifer attended with her shaved head, looking beautiful with the different bandanas she wore. She had a very good attitude, about her bald situation. A month later, Jennifer was nominated for homecoming queen, bald head and all!

Jennifer is now 31 years old, with two little girls of her own, and again, the Lord has kept her shunt working long past normal. She is a walking miracle of God. Every day, I ask myself, "Is God fair?" And I always answer, "No, God is not fair. He is more than fair!"

Things to Ponder

1. Scripture says "God works for the good of those who love Him." (Romans 8:28) Is this an easy thing to remember when things are going wrong in our lives?
2. "We cannot see the end results, so we focus on the things happening around us". Does a believer's focus get in God's way or the believer's way? How can the believer change his/her focus?
3. Jennifer's CT scan came back "normal" yet for her it was not "normal". Are things always as they appear? How should the believer handle those times which are not normal in his/her life?
4. Could it have been the voice of the Lord, prompting the neurosurgeon to have his nurse to check up on Jennifer? Does God really care about people?
5. "If God had not restored Jennifer's eyesight, He would still be God, and would be worthy of our praise." How do you feel about this statement?

6

Potholes of Life

The roads in our part of the world, have what we refer to as potholes. They are caused by water getting under the payment in the winter and then freezing. When the spring thaw comes, the ice thaws and goes into the ground leaving a void under the pavement. Then, when a car or truck drives over this spot, the pavement breaks up, creating a hole which we call a pothole. As time goes along, the hole gets bigger with each passing vehicle, until it is very large. Try as we may, it sometimes becomes very difficult to miss each and every one of these potholes. So it is with life. It is impossible to miss the potholes of troubles that come our way.

I have heard some preachers say that, if a person will just turn his or her life over to the Lord, everything will go well for them, but this just is not true. There are those who believe that, if a person is blessed with money, a good family, a good job, or something else, then that person must be living right with the Lord. Again, I must say that this is just not true. Look at Job; he had 7,000 sheep, 3000 camels, 500 yolk of oxen, 500 donkeys, and many servants. Then Satan challenged God that Job wouldn't be faithful, if he had hardships.

Notice what scripture says about this: Job 1:6-2:7

One day the angels came to present themselves before the LORD, and Satan also came with them. The LORD said to Satan, "Where have you come from?" Satan answered the LORD, "From roaming through the earth and going back and forth in it."
Then the LORD said to Satan, "Have you considered my servant Job? There is no one on earth like him; he is blameless and upright, a man who fears God and shuns evil."
"Does Job fear God for nothing?" Satan replied. "Have you not put a hedge around him and his household and

everything he has? You have blessed the work of his hands, so that his flocks and herds are spread throughout the land. But stretch out your hand and strike everything he has, and he will surely curse you to your face."

The LORD said to Satan, "Very well, then, everything he has is in your hands, but on the man himself do not lay a finger."

Then Satan went out from the presence of the LORD.

One day when Job's sons and daughters were feasting and drinking wine at the oldest brother's house, a messenger came to Job and said, "The oxen were plowing and the donkeys were grazing nearby, and the Sabeans attacked and carried them off. They put the servants to the sword, and I am the only one who has escaped to tell you!"

While he was still speaking, another messenger came and said, "The fire of God fell from the sky and burned up the sheep and the servants, and I am the only one who has escaped to tell you!"

While he was still speaking, another messenger came and said, "The Chaldeans formed three raiding parties and swept down on your camels and carried them off.

They put the servants to the sword, and I am the only one who has escaped to tell you!"

While he was still speaking, yet another messenger came and said, "Your sons and daughters were feasting and drinking wine at the oldest brother's house, when suddenly a mighty wind swept in from the desert and struck the four corners of the house. It collapsed on them and they are dead, and I am the only one who has escaped to tell you!"

On another day the angels came to present themselves before the LORD, and Satan also came with them to present himself before him. And the LORD said to Satan, "Where have you come from?" Satan answered the LORD, "From roaming through the earth and going back and forth in it." Then the LORD said to Satan, "Have you considered my servant Job? There is no one on earth like him; he is blameless and upright, a man who fears God and shuns evil. And he still maintains his integrity, though you incited me against him to ruin him without any reason." "Skin for skin!" Satan replied. "A man will give all he has for his own life. But stretch out your hand and strike his flesh and bones, and he will surely curse you to your face." The LORD said to Satan, "Very well, then, he is in your hands; but you must spare his life." So Satan went out from the presence of the LORD and afflicted Job with painful sores from the soles of his feet to the top of his head.

God allowed Satan to bring hardships upon Job, but through it all, Job remained faithful to the Lord God. Job's friends came and spent thirty some chapters trying to prove to Job that bad things don't happen to good people. In the end, God told Job that He would spare Job's friends, if Job prayed for them, which Job did. God then restored Job, with a new family and twice as much as He had before.

The apostle Paul also experienced the potholes of life. He talks about them in 2 Corinthians 11:23-28:

Are they servants of Christ? (I am out of my mind to talk like this.) I am more. I have worked much harder, been in prison more frequently, been flogged more severely, and been exposed to death again and again. Five times I received from the Jews the forty lashes minus one. Three times I was beaten with rods, once I was stoned, three times I was shipwrecked, I spent a night and a day in the open sea, I have been constantly on the move. I have been in danger from rivers, in danger from bandits, in danger from my own countrymen, in danger from Gentiles; in danger in the city, in danger in the country, in danger at sea; and in danger from false brothers. I have labored and toiled and have often gone without sleep; I have known hunger and thirst and have often gone without food; I have been cold and naked. Besides everything else, I face daily the pressure of my concern for all the churches.

You see, Satan hates you and wants to destroy you. He hates you for two reasons: Firstly he hates you because God created you in His own image. Satan hates God, so he hates everything that God created; especially mankind, because we were created in God's own image. Secondly, if you are truly a Christian, that is a person who has given Jesus lordship of his or her life, Satan hates you even more! His goal is to ruin your reputation, so that you will be ineffective for the Lord. Scripture says, in 1 Peter 5:8, "Your enemy the devil prowls around like a roaring lion looking for someone to devour". If he can get you to cry out against God, he thinks he has won, but God will forgive anything you do, if you just ask for forgiveness. The key to handling these potholes of life all reverts back to one's attitude, in dealing with these times.

Let me tell you about what happened to a man who was my own pastor several years ago. I first met Pastor Elmore Blain in 1986, while I was serving on the board of the Forsyth Wesleyan Church, in Forsyth, Montana. Our pastor had resigned, and we were searching for a new pastor. We had several qualified candidates, but none of them were exactly what God had in mind for us. Elmore, and his wife, Phyllis, were on the way to a church in the northwest part of Montana to candidate, but they agreed to stop by and meet with our board on their way.

We met with the Blains, and they left to continue on their trip. They had told us they were sure that they were going to take this other church, but they would pray about us as they traveled. The next thing we knew, Elmore was back in Forsyth as our pastor. Had I known what the next few years were going to be like for them, I would have told them to run as fast as they could away from us. There were some things in this church that needed to be dealt with, and Elmore was God's man to deal with them.

Just nine weeks into his new job at Forsyth, Elmore got a call one morning that a newly-married young couple was having difficulty. She had come home to her parents, who attended our church, and her husband had come after her, from the ranch about 60 miles away. The husband was trying to force his wife to go home with him. Elmore started his motorcycle and sped over to the parents' home, 10 miles away. He tried to quiet things down and encouraged the young man to go home. He told him that he would counsel his bride and try to get things worked out. Then, Elmore asked him to go home, and he said he would, so Elmore returned to the church.

It wasn't very long before the phone rang again; the young man had not left and the situation continued. When Elmore arrived, the sheriff was already there, so they both spoke with the young couple. Then, they took the young man out to lunch, instructed him to go on home, and assured him that they would keep working with her. Again, the young man said he would go home, so Elmore went back to the church. An hour or two later, Elmore received a third phone call; the young man was back, and the fight continued. Wasting no time, Elmore jumped onto his motorcycle and headed out, in a great big hurry. Only this time, he did not arrive at his destination. Instead, he woke up three days later in the hospital, with broken ribs, a broken neck, a punctured lung, a ruptured spleen, and a broken shoulder.

God had healed Elmore miraculously twice before; the first time was a back injury. He injured his back in high school doing something stupid, and then he re-injured it, in a sporting event. Later, just before he and Phyllis were married, Elmore worked on a ranch. That work involved a lot of tractor driving, which greatly affected his back. During an evening church service, his pastor said, "I feel like we need to pray for someone for healing". Elmore stood up and shared his story. "I don't know what else to do. I've been to chiropractors and my back is really causing me a lot of pain. I'd like to be prayed for." As he knelt at the altar, he had to hold himself really straight, because he couldn't bend his back. The pastor came over, put oil on his fingers, and laid his hand on Elmore's head. When he touched Elmore's head, his back snapped, and the pain was gone for good!

The second time Elmore received God's miraculous healing touch was on his knee. He had hurt that knee playing football when he was a sophomore in high school. He didn't have much trouble with it until in the '70s, when it really began to give him problems. He had four teenage boys, and his knee made it hard for him to do "boy things" with them.

That summer, he and his family were at Family Camp in Rapid City, and one evening there was a healing service. Elmore went forward and sat on the front pew. He didn't go forward to be anointed; he just sat there and prayed. "Lord, I've got these four boys to raise. I'd really appreciate it, if you'd help me with my knee." About six weeks later, it suddenly occurred to him that his knee wasn't bothering him anymore, and it still doesn't to this day. This was the second time God had healed Elmore, and now He was about to do it again.

The question might come to mind, would God heal Elmore again? God had something that He needed Elmore to accomplish, so He did indeed heal Elmore! Three doctors said he should have died, but God did a miracle, and instead Elmore lived.

While Elmore was in a coma, the Lord talked to him about two things. One was that he needed to learn to accept help graciously. Elmore was always a person who liked to be the one doing things, and now he needed to allow others to do things for him. He needed to humble himself and say, "Thank you, I appreciate that".

The other thing God spoke to Elmore about was an instruction to not change anything in the church for a year. By the end of that year, he knew what the problem was.

There was a couple in the church whose goal was to turn people against him. One time, this couple had my family over to their house for lunch after church, and John (not his real name) told me that "he was called by God, to get rid of the bad pastors of the Wesleyan church". I did not think about that again until I saw the things that this couple did to Elmore and Phyllis.

They had about 3 ½ years of living under a black cloud, and dealing with the things that happened. Besides his position as Pastor, Elmore was also a school bus driver. Each morning, when he drove out of town, the sun shone and he felt good. But, when he came to the end of the route, and turned around to head back toward town, it was like driving under a cloud.

One day, while some of the men were working in the sanctuary, John walked into Elmore's office. John called Elmore a "bastard" and spent a good part of an hour, explaining to him how he wasn't fit to be the pastor of the church. John spoke loud enough so the men working in the sanctuary could hear what he said. His plan was to make Elmore look bad in the eyes of the church.

The previous pastor had figured John out. He was able to get someone else elected as Sunday School Superintendent, just before Elmore came. At the next annual meeting, someone nominated John from the floor. He was reelected, and back on the board. This gave John some power, and he was able to cause even more problems for Pastor Elmore.

One Sunday after church, Elmore and Phyllis had an appointment to meet another pastor for lunch, in Miles City. They hurried home, went in the house for something, and came out to find John's wife, Sandy, (not her real name) parked in the ally, blocking their car. According to her, Elmore had made some terrible mistake, involving the music. She refused to accept his apology, and spent the next 30 minutes explaining to him, Phyllis, and several neighbors what an incompetent idiot he was.

At the same time all this was happening, there was also a man in the town who claimed to be a Satanist priest. He would put on his black garb and walk around church parking lots during worship services, with his incense, evoking Satan to destroy that church. One particular Sunday morning, Elmore felt choked and wasn't able to talk for a little bit. Somebody brought him a glass of water and he was able to continue with his message.

The time came to have a church trial for inveighing against the pastor. According to Roberts Rules of Order and the Wesleyan Discipline, two ordained elders and two laymen were selected as judges, one each, from four Wesleyan churches. John decided to go to work that day, so he was absent. Sandy sat and listened to evidence, but refused to comment. The four judges then went to another room, and soon returned with a unanimous decision to remove John and Sandy from the membership. John and Sandy called it a kangaroo court and refused to leave the church. However, they did leave their children home from church, so they would not be under Elmore's influence.

John and Sandy continued to attend, although they had been asked to leave. They would attend worship service, sit on the front pew and record each service looking for something to use against Elmore. Even after the removal of their church membership, they still tried to turn people against Pastor Elmore.

One Sunday, the board met them at the front door and asked them to stay out. Their response was "We're going to stand right here until you get out of the way, and then we're coming in." Their goal was now to disrupt the worship service in any way they could, trying to drive a wedge between the pastor and the congregation.

Later on, the church had revival services. The evangelist noticed that John was really troubled during the message. John and Sandy went home after the service and put their car away in the garage. Their 13-year old son was waiting in the garage with his dad's 357. He shot and killed his father right there in their garage; then he ran away. Sandy called 911, and Joan, a member of the church board, took the call. She told Joan what had happened, and then she said "are you happy now, Joan?"

About this time, Elmore got a phone call that there were gun shots at John and Sandy's house, and the sheriff was there. Soon the phone rang again, and Joan asked if she could come to the parsonage. She was crushed by the horror of it. Meanwhile the son had walked across town to a family friend, laid the gun on the table, and said "I killed John". He was taken to the sheriff's office, where he was locked up. Sandy soon went to the sheriff's office with a list of people who were not to be allowed to visit her son. The list included Elmore, along with the board members.

One would think that it would end with the death of John, but it did not. In the months to follow, Sandy continued to cause problems for Elmore and Phyllis. Sandy, and a friend, began to attend board meetings even though they were not on the board. Elmore called the meeting to order and asked if they had business. They said they didn't, but sat there with their recorder. Before the next meeting, Elmore checked Robert's Rules of Order, and found that they are not allowed to sit in a meeting, without invitation or pertinent business. When they showed up, he called the meeting to order, asked if they had business, which they didn't. At that point, he told them they needed to leave, and Sandy refused. He then asked for a motion to recess and reconvene at the parsonage, in ten minutes. He informed these ladies the parsonage was his home and they were not welcome there.

On the day John was killed, Elmore felt the Lord released him from the pastorate there, in Forsyth. He finished that year, resigned, and did not take a full time pastorate again. Since this time, the average attendance of this church has dropped to less than half of what it was.

Even after leaving this church, Elmore's pot holes of life did not end. Shortly before they moved, they were on a trip with one of their sons, and his wife, to the wedding of another son. On the way home, this son and wife became very upset with something that Elmore had done. He was accused of not doing right, even though he had just done what he had been asked to do. This son and his wife spent an hour, yelling at Elmore and Phyllis, as they rode with them in their car. They informed Elmore and Phyllis that they were stupid parents, unfair, and that they treated the other boys better than they treated them.

Elmore and Phyllis moved to the town where this son lived. The son, who was a minister, left the denomination that Elmore and Phyllis had been part of all of their lives and decided to go independent. He became a dictator of the church that he pastored. He didn't have a board, and made all the decisions himself. Elmore showed him biblically, that what he was doing wasn't right. At that point, his son told him, "Get out of my house and don't ever come back". Elmore and Phyllis lived just five blocks away. The son had three little girls, and another one was born shortly after that. For over three years, Elmore and Phyllis were not even able to see their grandchildren.

They are still working through another pothole of life. About a year and a half ago, Elmore noticed that his right hand was becoming quite weak. He had a handyman business and was busy working all day, on a regular basis, but he was losing strength. His doctor looked at it, and said there was definitely something wrong. Elmore had an MRI, and then surgery on his neck, to relieve a pinched nerve, but the hand continued to deteriorate. About six or eight months later, it was determined that he had Amyotrophic Lateral Sclerosis (ALS) commonly known as Lou Gehrig's disease. This disease causes a loss of strength in arms and legs. Its victims eventually die of pneumonia, when the lungs quit functioning.

No one knows God's plan. All we know is that He is in charge, and that He will work out His will, in His perfect time. Elmore has been anointed with oil and prayed for, but God hasn't chosen to heal him, at this point. He may or may not; that's His business. We only know that He's given Elmore grace for the difficult times.

Scripture says in Phil 2:14-15, 4:4

Do everything without complaining or arguing, so that you may become blameless and pure, children of God without fault in a crooked and depraved generation, in which you shine like stars in the universe. 4:4, Rejoice in the Lord always. I will say it again: Rejoice!

It is easy to blame God when a person goes through these types of potholes of life, and give up on God, but He never gives up on us. Is He fair? No, He is more than fair! Elmore would tell you that through everything, God has been with him. On February 16, 2012 Elmore won the crown of life and heard the Lord say to him, "Well done, good and faithful servant!"

Things to Ponder

1. Some preachers say that, if a person will just turn his or her life over to the Lord, everything will go well for them. Is this true or false? How do you feel about this?
2. In the book of Job, God asks Satan "have you considered my servant Job?" It appears that God is bragging about Job, is this the case?
3. God miraculously healed Elmore two times. Why do you think God did not heal him from ALS?
4. Why is it that some people purposely try to drive a wedge between the pastor and the congregation?
5. When it seems that there is nothing a person can do, where should that person turn?

7

In The Shelter of His Wings

Wouldn't we all like to feel a hedge of protection around us? We do not want anything to come our way that might hurt us, but things do happen and we do get hurt. When things happen, we can always take shelter under God's wings. David talks about this in the Psalms. In Psalms 61:1-4, he says:

> Hear my cry, O God; listen to my prayer. From the ends of the earth I call to you, I call as my heart grows faint; lead me to the rock that is higher than I. For you have been my refuge, a strong tower against the foe. I long to

dwell in your tent forever and take refuge in the shelter of your wings.

It is said that August Toplady was caught in a storm, and took refuge in a cave in the rocks. As he waited out the storm, he thought about the storms of life that come our way, and about the only One in Whom we can find shelter. He then wrote the words to the first verse of "Rock of Ages", on a playing card. Over the years, this beloved hymn has been a source of strength in the lives of many believers.

My friend Dianna Miller is one person who knows, without a doubt, that she can take refuge in the shelter of God's wings. The following is her story of what happened in May of 1992.

It was just a week before Dianna's high school graduation. Her friend, Timber Harkins, was a young pilot and had flown her sister and grandmother to Troy, Montana, from the Missoula airport, two days earlier. Diana had wanted to take a plane ride with him, but it had never worked out. This time she was a little more persistent, and Timber finally agreed to take her, and her mom, for a ride in his plane. After going with the youth group to Kootenai Falls, on Sunday, May 24, 1992, they headed back into Troy, for their flight.

Dianna's father was the director of camp Elohim, which is located just south of Troy, Montana, and about a mile from Bull Lake. Their plan was to fly up Lake Creek, which would have lead right to Bull Lake, then turn and follow the highway back over the camp. Dianna sat in the co-pilot seat, and her mom, Pam, sat in the back of Timber's four- passenger Cessna. They took off to the west, circled around, came back across the town, heading up what they thought was Lake Creek.

They would learn a few days later that they were actually starting up Callahan Creek. As they flew along, Timber asked Pam and Dianna if they recognized anything. It didn't look quite like he though it should. But this was the view from the air, not from on the road, and it would look different from up there. So they continued. Had they been going up Lake Creek, there would have been very little change in altitude, so they flew quite low. Callahan Creek lead them into a box canyon and they gained elevation.

Timber realized then, that they were in trouble, so he decided to turn around. In attempting that, they hit a tree and crashed into the forest below. Dianna was the first one to wake up. She found Timber's head on her shoulder, and woke him. They were both in shock. Dianna's first instinct was to get out. She opened the plane door and fell out three to four feet to the ground. When she hit the ground with a thud, pain shot through her. She later learned the cause of that pain was that her 4th lumbar vertebrae and both feet were broken.

At the same time, Timber had tried to wake up Pam, but she was already gone. Her broken rib had severed her aorta, so death came very quickly. Timber got her out of the plane; then came around to check on Dianna. All this time, Dianna knew deep down, that her mother had not survived the crash. Dianna had gotten herself up on the wheel of the plane, but the pain was just too much; she slid back to the ground.

Timber had crushed his jaw, and there was a lot of blood on his face. He also had a broken ankle and a hairline fracture in the other leg. But, even though he was in shock, and had a lot of pain, he knew that he had to get help. It was late in the day; he laced up his high top shoes, told Dianna goodbye, and began to hobble through the woods.

In tee shirts and shorts, neither Timber, nor Dianna, were dressed for the ordeal that they were about to go through. At least Timber had a hat that he had bought on a recent trip to Australia. It would come in handy for drinking water from the creek, as he made his way looking for help. Dressed like this in the mountains of western Montana, where there was still snow on the ground, they both faced the possibility of dying from hypothermia.

Hypothermia is a condition resulting from the loss of body temperature required for metabolism and body functions. When a person's body temperature drops, they shiver and become confused. If the temperature continues to fall, they have difficulty speaking and thinking. Major organs stop working and the end will come with death.

That first night, Dianna slept underneath one wing of the plane, the other wing was destroyed in the crash. Timber, on the other hand, huddled up under a tree, put his arms inside his tee shirt, and shivered.

Dianna was in and out of consciousness and dreamed of a stack of blankets. She woke up every so often to the sound of breaking branches. The mountains of western Montana are the home to grizzly bears, black bears, mountain lions and wolves. All of these would be attracted to the smell of blood, and could have decided that one or both of these people, were to be their next meal. But, Dianna and Timber were both under the protection of God's wings, and no animals came near them.

The next morning (Monday), Dianna was very cold, so she tried to move out from underneath the wing of the plane, into the sunshine, for some warmth. This was not an easy task, but she had found a stick to help her. She did not have to move very far, but every inch took enormous effort, and caused her more pain.

While resting in the sunshine, a mouse rustled near her head. She then said to it, "Ok, really I don't need to deal with you right now; you need to leave. I have enough problems of my own, go away." Sure enough, it went away and was gone for several hours.

Sometime later, the mouse returned and began pushing on the bottoms of Dianna's feet. They were both pretty much crushed, so this caused her more pain. It just kept on pushing on her feet, time and time again. This little mountain mouse, as she called it, put pressure on her feet and it really hurt. She then decided, if it was not going to leave her alone, she would move; so she scooted back up underneath the wing of the plane. Just as she got underneath the wing of the plane it started to rain.

Dianna had made a cone cup out of a page of an aviation book that had fallen out of the plane when she had opened the door following the crash. She then made a hole in the ground, placed the cone cup in the hole to catch the water that dripped off the wing she sat under. Unfortunately she was only able to get a couple of tablespoons of water the whole time she sat there. So by the end of her time there she was not only dreaming of a stack of blankets, but she was also dreaming of a mega tanker of Sprite.

Had she remained where she was, she would have been drenched by the cold rain, resulting in considerable loss in body temperature. With her broken bones, she would not have been able to warm herself back up, by moving around. This would have been another chance for hypothermia to set in.

That same day, Timber found himself in a clearing when a plane flew overhead. He thought to himself, that the emergency locater beacon must have gone off in the plane, and a rescue party would find them shortly. He sat on a log in the clearing for quite a while, watching for that plane to come back around, but it never did. What a disappointment!

They later learned that the emergency beacon had been turned off during the last inspection, and had not been turned back on, so, it didn't activate in the crash. People came from all over to search, but the trouble was, they were searching in the wrong area. They searched in the area the plane was supposed to be, the Lake Creek area, but the plane went down in the Callahan Creek area. One of the many searchers was Dianna's childhood friend. He lost his job, because of his decision to join the search.

On Tuesday, it drizzled all day long, and Timber didn't cover much ground. He was very cold so he huddled under a big fir tree and tried to stay warm. Dianna was safe under the wing of the plane, at the same time.

When we are forced to 'stay put' for whatever reason, we have no choice but to just sit and think. This gives the Lord a chance to speak to our heart, and so He did to Dianna. She began to think of different stories that Pat Anderson used to tell them, at summer camp (Trails End Ranch, Ekalaka Montana). Every night at chapel, she told a story. They were earthly stories, with heavenly meanings; the campers called them 'Pat's parables'.

Dianna remembered one of these stories: A prairie fire raced across the ranchland, fueled by a mighty wind. In an effort to protect his home and livestock, a rancher plowed a fire line, making sure that all the animals were on the inside of the line. The fire burned its way around his ranch and the next day he went out to survey the damage. As he walked past the fire line, he found a lump on the ground. In his discouragement at the site of all that had burned, he kicked that lump, and out from underneath came a bunch of little chicks.

The mother chicken had known that the fire was coming, and she had gathered her chicks to her. She protected them from the fire, as they took refuge under her wings.

Dianna realized that God used the wing of that plane to give her refuge — to shelter her from the storm. She was reassured that the Lord was watching over her and keeping her safe. A verse of scripture repeated in her mind: "When I am afraid, I will trust in you". (Psalms 56:3) Dianna knew she was still there for a reason and God had a plan for her life.

Dianna had a lot of time to think about different things. She played songs in her head, from songs of praise to the Lord, to the song she was to sing at her graduation, the following week. These things kept her mind occupied, so that she did not give into fear, which would have been very easy.

All this time, Timber continued to make his way back down Callahan Creek. He found a stick, to help himself walk. He had that brand new hat that he had gotten from Australia, which he really prized. He did not want to ruin it; after all it was something that helped him remember that trip. At first, he tried kneeling down on the ground to drink directly from the creek, but his knees were badly cut, and the creek bank was covered with sharp rocks. After one attempt to kneel and drink, he decided that the hat would make a pretty good drinking cup!

He tried chewing on pine needles to satisfy his hunger, but they were so bitter that he couldn't bear to get them on his tongue. Somewhere along the creek, he came across a rotten log, which had a lot of big ants on it and he feasted on them. He had to pinch the head of these ants before he ate them; otherwise they would have bitten him on his tongue.

Over the days, Timber had followed the creek through the dense forest, for about seven miles. Then, on Thursday morning, he decided to cross the creek. Over the embankment, and found a logging road. He spotted a mile marker with a 3 on it, and thought that he was only three miles from town; it was actually farther than that. This motivated him to walk a little faster down that road.

He was about 100 yards from a fork in the road when he saw a truck with loggers going up the other fork. One of the loggers saw him, and they turned back. They had heard the news of the plane crash, so they had an idea of who Timber was. The men helped Timber into the truck and drove him back to the Troy hospital, where the rescue workers were alerted to Dianna's whereabouts.

In The Shelter Of His Wings

That same morning Dianna decided to try to get herself out. She used a stick to push herself out from under the wing of the plane. At one point, she even stood up, but immediately fell back over. This, in itself, should have probably caused paralysis, but it didn't. When a search plane flew over, she made her way out from under the wing and waved her stick. But, as the pilot flew over, unaware, she thought, "Wait a minute, hello, I'm still down here."

Soon, he came back over her and she could see the pilot, as he waved at her. Breathing a sigh of relief, she knew she had been found. About 10 minutes later, an air force helicopter hovered overhead. A rescue worker was lowered in a basket; he helped her into it and up they went. Once inside the helicopter, the emergency personnel began to ask her questions, which made no sense to her.

Of course, she knew what year it was and who the president was. "Why are they asking me these stupid questions," she wondered, not realizing that they were checking for brain damage. Dianna had been in a plane crash, and out in the cold for five days, yet her brain was just fine, for she had been under the shelter of God's wings.

Then she told her rescuers about her high school graduation scheduled for Sunday. "Am I going to be able to make it?" she asked. "Yeah, you'll make it," was the response. And she did make it, but not that Sunday, it would not be until months later.

When she arrived at the hospital in Libby, MT, her dad was waiting for her. She was so happy to see him, yet she knew she had to tell him the bad news. "Dad, Mom didn't make it."

The hospital crew made an assessment of Dianna's injuries; soon she was on a plane to Spokane, WA, where they would be better equipped to deal with her injuries. There, she spent the night with her feet elevated. She was not given anything to drink, which did not make her very happy, because she had been dreaming of a mega tanker of Sprite for days.

Next, Dianna was flown to Harborview Medical Center, in Seattle, where she underwent two back surgeries, and a surgery on each foot. She spent about a month there, and had a few special visitors: Bob and Pat Anderson, from Trails End Ranch, Ekalaka Montana, who left staff training to be with her.

Another visitor was one of her teachers, who brought along her diploma, but she refused to accept it. With her most determined voice, Dianna said, "No, I'm going to walk up and get it just like everybody else." These visits made a big impact on Dianna.

When people spend time in a hospital with serious injuries, it seems that they are constantly poked and prodded. Some staff members have a gentle touch; they seem to understand the pain of their patients. One nurse named Anne has a special place in Dianna's heart. It could be because of the tenderness in her touch that Dianna remembers Anne, but I think it's because Anne allowed Jesus to love Dianna through her.

Jesus says in John 13:35 "By this all men will know that you are my disciples, if you love one another". Here, Jesus is not talking just about showing love to fellow believers, but to all our fellow human beings. Every believer is given opportunities to show the love of Jesus to our fellow man, but many of us fail in this regard. However, a few believers make this a central part of their lives, and the impact they have on their fellow man is tremendous.

After all her surgeries, Dianna was released home. She had an ambulance ride from Seattle, WA, back to Troy, MT. What she remembers about that ride, other than it was long, was that one of the ambulance attendants spent a lot of time talking with her. They interacted, and even did some word searches, which made time pass smoothly.

Dianna spent most of the rest of the summer in a hospital bed, in the living room of their home. There she experienced the love of many different people, as they took wonderful care of her. There was always a lot of activity, as campers and staff came to visit.

In August, she started rehabilitation, at St. Luke's hospital in Spokane, WA. It was a very hard month. She had to learn to walk again, which was not an easy process. The first time she sat up in bed and let her feet dangle over the edge, she felt tremendous pain, as the blood rushed back to her feet. At first, each step was like walking on pins and needles.

Also, her time at St. Luke's was very lonely. At home, friends and family made for constant activity, but at the hospital she spent many hours by herself. Dianna spent this time thinking and mourning. She shed many tears as she dealt with the loss of her mom. Finally, Dianna was able to return home, walking with crutches.

On her first night home, Dianna and her sister, Pam, sang the national anthem at the high school football game. Then, during half time at the homecoming basketball game, Dianna walked across the gym floor, in cap and gown, with her crutches, to receive her high school graduation diploma. At this, the crowd stood. . . and the applause was deafening!

In The Shelter Of His Wings

I visited with Dianna, in September, 2011, at Camp Bighorn, near Plains, MT, where she is the office manager, and I could see nothing that would indicate that she had been hurt. The doctors had told her that she would never walk again, but as we walked around the camp she did not even limp!

Dianna is a prime example of the saying, "your walk talks louder than your talk, talks." At her ten year high school reunion, a class mate commented on the impact of Dianna's life. "I just want you to know it's because of how you've lived your life, that I am who I am today."

I am sure that Dianna would tell you that it is not the peaceful times that produce great trust in God, but it is the journey through the storms of life that does. You see, God does not save us out of those storms of life, but He walks with us through those storms. To this, I would have to say again, "God is not fair, He is more than fair!"

Things to Ponder

1. Where is the only place the believer can find shelter during times of trouble? Is there a time you can remember when you found that shelter?
2. Both Dianna and Timber faced the possibility of dying from hypothermia, why do you think this did not come to pass?
3. A mouse began pushing on the bottoms of Dianna's feet. What made the mouse do this and was there a purpose in it doing this?
4. Dianna had a few special visitors while she was in the hospital. How would this have been an encouragement for her? Have you ever done this for someone outside of your immediate family or friends?
5. "Every believer is given opportunities to show the love of Jesus to our fellow man, but many of us fail in this regard." Why do some fail and others do not?

8

Guiding Light

When I was in my thirties, I liked to get up before sunrise, and walk in the hills that surrounded our home. I always enjoyed those mornings, as I walked across the hills using no artificial light, but just walking by the light of the moon and stars. Then I would sit and wait for the wild creatures to walk by; they did not know that I was there. Had I used a flashlight, I would have alerted them to my presence.

Now that I am older, I find that I need a light, so that I can see the pathway. In scripture the Lord has provided a light to lead His people. In the Old Testament the Lord Himself was the guiding light for the children of Israel, as they traveled through the wilderness. He led them this way, so there would be no doubt which way they were to go.

One of the purposes of the Bible is to show people the path on which they are to travel through life. If a person were to spend time reading the Bible, they would find a lot of things that they could apply to their lives. In fact the Bible says, in Psalms 119:105, "Your word is a lamp to my feet and a light for my path".

This is a lesson that Tom and Karen Cobb have learned in their lives, following the Lord. They are General Evangelists in the Wesleyan Church and travel throughout the USA and Canada sharing from the Word of God (Bible). For more than 40 years, they have done ministry on the road.

One year, early in February, Tom and Karen had services scheduled in Gillette, Wyoming. It turned out that the weather was very cold that weekend, with temperatures dropping to 25 degrees below zero Fahrenheit, at night. This made it extremely difficult to stay warm in their motorhome, which was not designed for that kind of weather. They had hung extra blankets over the doors and windows, in an effort to keep the cold out. Even the water dish for their daughter's cat froze at night.

To complicate matters even more, their refrigerator wasn't working properly. While everything inside of the motorhome was freezing, their food in the freezer compartment was thawing out. Just a few days earlier, Tom had hired a refrigeration expert to check the RV refrigerator. After a careful inspection, the repairman had informed Tom that he could not fix this refrigerator.

It seems that an RV refrigerator is charged with ammonia, rather than Freon, which is used in household refrigerators. If the ammonia somehow leaked out, it could not be replaced, so even with the thermostat set at its lowest setting, the refrigerator would not cool. The repairman had suggested that they discard the old one and just buy a new one. Tom checked his RV catalog and found that a new one would cost around $1200. That was way out of his price range.

Karen had removed everything from the refrigerator, placed it in a box and placed the box next to the door. She knew that nothing would spoil in the frigid temperature of the motorhome. That night all the family was snuggled under their warm blankets, except Karen, who was reading from her Bible. Without warning, she turned to Tom and told him that he could fix their refrigerator, if he really wanted to. He could not believe what he heard; after all, he had just had the best repairman in the area tell him that it couldn't be fixed.

Tom had not slept very well the night before, because the wind rocked the motorhome back and forth. On top of that, he worried that the cold temperatures would freeze the water lines, which would mean countless hours to thaw them out. He would really rather be somewhere that he did not have to deal with this cold weather. All this added together, caused him to feel offended by her statement. Satan just loves it when he can drive a wedge between two believers, and he must have enjoyed Tom's reaction.

Tom jumped out of bed, grabbed some tools, and headed outside, without even bothering to grab his coat. There he stood, outside in his pajamas, in the freezing cold, thinking "she just doesn't appreciate me, but when I get back inside shivering and cold, at least then she'll feel sorry for me."

As he stared into the refrigerator compartment, he suddenly received a gift of knowledge from God, like he had never received before. Somehow, he just knew what was causing the problem with the refrigerator. He turned a few screws, and checked a few wires. Then, he used the end of the screwdriver to clean some soot away from the orifice. Instantly the flame, which heated the refrigerator's coil, turned from a strange yellow to a lovely blue, and he knew that the refrigerator was fixed.

He had been outside for only a few minutes, and was not even cold. But the job was finished, so he returned inside. As he stepped through the door, Karen said, "You fixed it, didn't you?" She wasn't scolding him; she was just stating a fact. She had just been reading Philippians 4:13, which says, "I can do everything through him who gives me strength". Instead of Satan driving a wedge between them, they rejoiced in the Lord, because they had both experienced the same connection with the Holy Spirit!

God makes it possible for believers to do things that we do not come by naturally. The Bible is full of His promises that are available to all believers. Our only connection to them is through reading His Word, and applying it to our lives. But God also speaks directly to our spirits, with that still, small voice.

Another time, Tom and Karen were in South Dakota, preparing to travel from Rapid City to Prairie City. Tom had ordered some tires for their motorhome, and they were having them put on at a tire shop, before they left.

They had a trailer that they pulled behind their motorhome. The positioning of the hitch put the tongue of the trailer at just the right height to trip over. Tom just couldn't seem to miss tripping over the tongue of the trailer, each time he walked past it that day. He must have tripped over it a half dozen times.

Although they did not need to be in Prairie City until the next day, they started out after lunch expecting to arrive a day early. As they drove along they talked about many things. Then, their conversation took a turn, as Karen asked Tom about a theological issue. They soon discovered that they had opposing views, and a heated argument ensued.

As they drove down a hill, Tom noticed a two-wheeled trailer, in his mirror, about to pass them. He was so engrossed in the argument, that at first he didn't pay any attention. Then, the thought hit him — it was their trailer, and he was certain that it was about to crash into the ditch! For just a moment, it appeared that he was wrong. The trailer stayed on a course parallel to them.

Then, it made a shift to the left, and its tongue dug into the soft soil at the edge of the highway. This brought the trailer to a sudden stop, breaking the upper portion of the trailer apart, and spewing all their equipment through the roadside fence and into a cow pasture. As they watched in dismay, guitars, speakers, record albums, and even Karen's sewing machine, flew through the air landing in a cloud of dust.

They pulled to the side of the highway, and began to pick up their equipment. The highway was littered with loose record albums, cassette tapes, microphones and cables. They soon heard a car approaching. It stopped, and the driver gave them a hand clearing the highway. About ten minutes after he left, another car with two women arrived, as the family gathered up the rest of their equipment, and placed it in piles alongside the road.

The two asked if they needed any help. Karen began to explain what had happened, when one of these ladies asked, "Are you the Cobbs?" She had recognized them from a dedication service they had taken part in, at the Rainbow Bible Camp, a year earlier. This lady then said she would call her husband, John, and ask him to come with his flat-bed trailer. She said that John would haul all of the Cobb's things to their farm, and possibly even help Tom fix the trailer.

They arrived at the farm around 5:30 PM, and Tom immediately began to check their equipment, to see how badly damaged it was. Their most expensive piece of equipment was a portable electric grand piano, so they started with it. This piano cost them over four thousand dollars, and it required professional tuning, from time to time. Parts of it had landed far beyond the fence, which would have been like dropping it from a second story window. They assembled the piano, tried it out, and found that it still played beautiful tones.

Their amplifier had a crack along the top of its wooden frame, but the components inside were unbroken. As they tested each piece of equipment, they found that in spite of the dust and damage, everything worked just as it should. I can just imagine a group of angels, flying around catching the flying equipment and gently setting it on the ground, while stirring up dust to make it seem real.

They were still awe struck with the lack of damage to their equipment, when they were introduced to John's mother, who invited them to dinner. As they entered the house, the aroma of an elaborate meal struck them. There were fried chicken, fresh baked rolls, mashed potatoes, gravy and three types of pie.

Karen could see that John's mother had prepared this meal for company, and she felt they might be putting someone else out. But, John's mother explained that she had prepared this meal especially for them. She went on to tell them, that each morning she has a quiet time with the Lord, reading her Bible and praying. She had not planned to spend much time in the kitchen, as the day had already started out to be a warm one. Then, during her prayer time, the Lord had told her to prepare a special meal that night, because they would be having company. She didn't know who would arrive, but she trusted that God knew.

After that great meal, Tom, John and John's father went to the shop, and began repairing the demolished trailer. By midnight, it was completely rebuilt, ready to hitch to the motorhome, and reload with their equipment. The next morning they were back on the road, headed for Prairie City.

Tom was quite impressed by John's mother's connection with the Lord; especially her ability to know and act upon His directives. Tom began to follow her example of spending more of his time reading from God's Word, praying, and listening for His direction.

One day, he asked the Lord why He had spoken to John's mother about preparing for their arrival, about the same time he was tripping over the tongue of the trailer. Why had He not just told Tom about the problem with the trailer, rather than having them go to this family's home? God's response was not what Tom wanted to hear. The Lord told him that He had spoken to both of them, but Tom was not listening.

God still speaks to people, but so many times people don't listen. We get so caught up in the cares of this world, that is, the things we think are important, that we do not take time to listen for that still, small voice of God.

When Jesus was asked what the greatest commandment was, He responded, "Love the Lord your God with all your heart and with all your soul and with all your strength and with all your mind." and "Love your neighbor as yourself". (Luke 10:27) When Jesus was asked, "Who is my neighbor?" He answered by telling the story of the Good Samaritan. The Samaritans were just part Jewish and were hated by the Jewish people.

We, as Christians, know that we are to love our neighbors as ourselves, but sometimes we have a hard time doing this, depending on who those 'neighbors' are. Some of the most difficult to love are those who try to take away something we believe is ours. Let me share with you another thing that happened to Tom and Karen Cobb:

They had been out on the road, proclaiming the love of Jesus, only to return home to find a letter from the IRS, stating that they owed $8600 in back taxes. The letter went on to explain that if, they didn't send a check immediately, their situation would get worse. The letter included two phone numbers to call, if they had any questions, or wanted to talk to an agent, who could explain this situation to them. Tom tried calling, but was not able to get through to anyone.

The letter came from the IRS office in North Platte, Nebraska, and the Cobbs were already scheduled to travel through there, in a few days. Tom decided to stop by the office and see if he could talk to someone there. He also called his accountant, who thought the IRS was wrong, but really didn't give Tom much assurance. He told Tom that whenever the IRS is this confident about a case, they almost always get something from the taxpayer.

On the day they were headed for North Platte, they stopped at their mail box, to find another letter from the IRS, stating they now owed an additional $600. As they traveled, Karen read Psalms 91:1-2 "He who dwells in the shelter of the Most High will rest in the shadow of the Almighty. I will say of the LORD, "He is my refuge and my fortress, my God, in whom I trust". They knew that the Lord was with them in this matter.

Just a few months before, the Federal Building in Oklahoma City had been bombed and hundreds of people had been killed. Our country was in fear of something like that happening again, and it could be seen by Tom and Karen, as they entered the IRS office, in North Platte. There was no receptionist. Instead, on the wall next to the locked door was a button, with a sign telling visitors, if they wished to talk to someone inside, they should push the button. A short time after they pushed the button, they heard a man's voice, asking who they were and what they wanted.

Sensing the tension, Tom explained their purpose, in the calmest manner he could, and a man opened the door, looking out at them. Then, he ushered them into a small room, piled with boxes and papers. On the other side of the room was a woman seated at a desk, half covered with papers.

Without looking up, she told them she would be with them in a few minutes. She asked them to excuse the mess. With Government cut-backs, they could not afford to hire a secretary for her anymore.

Tom and Karen felt compassion for this lady, who seemed to be drowning in a sea of bureaucratic paper work. When she finished her task and looked up, prepared to hear their complaint, Tom felt that his problems didn't seem as important to him as hers did. Tom and Karen talked to her about her work for some time, asking how she coped with the pressures. They sympathized with her having to compensate for a shrinking budget.

When Tom remembered the reason for their visit, he didn't want to take up any more of her time, and explained that they were there to set up an appointment with someone to discuss the additional taxes the IRS requested. She set up an appointment, and told him the particular records and receipts he should bring back with him, that might help his position.

When they arrived home, Tom called his accountant and asked him to go to the appointment they had set up with the IRS auditor. The accountant was happy to attend, but was concerned that Tom and Karen had already talked with her and discussed their situation. The accountant told him that talking to her was not a very good idea, as the first impression made upon an IRS agent often sets the tone for the case, which indeed it did.

Later, when they arrived for their appointment with the IRS auditor, Tom and Karen were prepared with their records and receipts. Whenever the auditor asked for a particular receipt, he was able to produce it. At one point, the auditor picked up the phone and called the office in Omaha, Nebraska, to discuss the case. When she hung up the phone, she announced that they would not receive any more notices from the IRS, demanding payment, as she had put a freeze on the account.

As the appointment came to an end, Tom asked her if that meant that they didn't owe the government ninety-two hundred dollars. The auditor chuckled, as she told them that they did not owe anything; and as a matter of fact, it looked like they would be getting around two thousand dollars back!

The thing is, how we treat a person is reflected back, in how that person treats us in return. The golden rule is to "do to others as you would have them do to you", (Luke 6:31) but I think, as a believer, we should treat others better than we want to be treated. Love does things for others out of a pure heart, expecting nothing in return.

Through the years, Tom and Karen have become more and more sensitive to the leading of the Holy Spirit. Whenever they both have a sense of the same leading, they have learned to be very submissive to it.

Once, when they were in Salina, Kansas, they both had the feeling that they should head south. So they began driving south on Interstate 135, not sure where they were going, but sure they were following the leading of the Holy Spirit. They hadn't traveled very far, when a semi-truck passed them, and the driver motioned to Tom to turn on his CB radio.

As he did, Tom heard the trucker say that he had been driving for quite a while. The trucker was bored and just wanted someone to talk to. As they talked, Tom began to share some of the things that had happened to them, as they traveled the highways for the Lord.

He shared that, one time they were traveling in Arizona, with a truck and fifth wheel trailer rig they had, at that time. They had pulled into a rest area on a hill, to take in the breathtaking view of the valley below. They were parked just a short distance from a cliff, which was a few hundred feet to the bottom. While Tom was out with their children, taking some pictures, Karen began preparing sandwiches in the fifth wheel trailer, which was still attached to their truck.

Karen noticed that the trailer was making some unusual noises, but thought it was from things cooling down. Then she looked out the window, and saw scenery going by! Driven by panic, she ran out the door, hoping to outrun the truck and trailer, get into the truck, and stop it from going over the cliff. She caught up with the truck, and jumping on the running board, she opened the passenger door, to find an elderly gentleman seated behind the wheel, applying the brakes!

This truck was not the typical pickup that most people use, but a beefed up, specially built truck, with a different type of braking system. The brakes were hydraulic with a backup electric motor. In order for the brakes to work, the motor needed to be running, or at least the key had to be turned on. Neither was the case, so the brakes should not have worked. But as this man pushed on the brakes, the truck and trailer stopped! Karen had no idea who this man was, or how he got into the truck. He never stopped to introduce himself. He simply got into a car, with Minnesota plates, and drove away. Either this man was a very humble, caring person, who was willing to risk his life to help people he didn't even know, or one has to wonder if angels ever drive cars with Minnesota plates. God's hand was definitely at work in their lives that day!

As Tom told that story, he felt the Spirit telling him it was time to turn onto another road. So, he offered to pray with this trucker, and bid him goodbye. The last thing Tom heard the trucker say was, even though he had not been much of a churchgoer, he would definitely be in church the next Sunday!

One thing that more believers need to learn is, not to be afraid of sharing their faith. Imagine how many other people heard that conversation that day, and were touched by it. Again, I must say "God is not fair, He is more than fair."

Some Good Advice:

Spend time in His Word every day. Look for the promises He makes. Then look for what God is doing in your own life, and tell others about it!

Things to Ponder

1. The Bible says, in Psalms 119:105, "Your word is a lamp to my feet and a light for my path". Can a person make the Word of God a lamp to follow and if so how?
2. Philippians 4:13 says, "I can do everything through him who gives me strength". Is there a limit to what the believer can do through God?
3. Why does it seem that God speaks to just a few "privileged" people? Are you listening for the voice of the Lord?
4. "Love does things for others out of a pure heart, expecting nothing in return." Have you ever put that into action?
5. Tom shared a story over the CB radio as he drove down the highway. I am sure that more people heard that story as he drove. Is it a good idea to tell stories of faith where others can hear them?

9

Divine Appointments

A testimony to the Lord is always uplifting for everyone who hears it. As a Pastor of small churches, on Sunday mornings, I would ask the congregation what the Lord has done in their lives during the past week. I wanted them to recognize even the small things that the Lord is doing in their lives, and by doing that, to begin to look for the Hand of the Lord daily.

The trouble is that most Christians do not see the Lord's handprint in their daily lives. We hear about the mighty things He does in the lives of some people, like rescuing them from a great tragedy. This leads us to think that if He isn't doing something great, He isn't doing anything at all.

But, if we look closely, we can see the Hand of the Lord God, working in the small areas of our lives, as well.

When trouble comes, instead of resting in the Lord and relying on His perfect plan, we search for answers from other sources. When one doesn't work, we move on to another. . .and then another. . .in an endless search to fix the trouble. This rush of confusion reminds me of a scene in the first Star Wars movie, when Luke is making his final run to destroy the Death Star. Darth Vader comes up behind Luke to take him out, but Luke's friends shoot Darth Vader's craft and it goes spinning out of control.

A similar thing happens when Satan brings tribulation into the lives of Christian people. If we do not rely on the Lord, we can go spinning out of control. But it doesn't have to be that way. If we, as Christians, would prepare ahead of time, through prayer, the outcome would be very different.

I asked my friend, Karen Lorenz, of Helena, Montana, what was the most exciting thing God had done in her life. She readily responded with a personal story of God's angels of protection, and she believes that protection is available to all Christians, if we just ask God for it. Karen and her husband always pray, before every trip, for God to place angels on the four corners of their vehicle.

Divine Appointments

On the evening of January 7, 1998, her grandson, Trevor John, was born. Karen, along with her pastor's wife, Sue Ann, had driven to Bozeman, so they could be there for the baby's birth. Shortly after he was born, it started to snow, so they left Bozeman, about 9:00 PM, and headed back to Helena, about one hundred miles away.

By the time they reached Three Forks, the snow had increased, and they found themselves driving through three or four inches of slush. Karen drove, keeping her car in the ruts created by the vehicles ahead of them. As she looked ahead, she could see two semis pulled over on the right side of the road. With the slush and snow, she assumed the truck drivers were putting chains on their trucks.

Suddenly Karen saw one of the truck drivers walking down the middle of her lane. She immediately changed lanes, which caused her car to start spinning down the highway. There were sharp drop offs on both sides of that highway, but they ended up in the right lane facing the right direction!

Both Karen and Sue Ann gasped and said, "Did you see them?" They asked each other if either of them had seen the angels God had sent to protect them, by steering the car! They continued home, seeing several vehicles in the ditches all the way along, but they knew without a doubt that God was in control and had His Hand on their lives.

That was definitely an exciting time in Karen's life, but what I see in that night, is a picture of Karen's walk with the Lord. When Satan brings tribulation into her life, instead of spinning out of control, she allows God to bring her back onto the path He has set for her.

In Proverbs 3:5-6, the Lord says, "Trust in the LORD with all your heart and lean not on your own understanding; in all your ways acknowledge him, and he will make your paths straight". This is a lesson that Karen has learned. I know it was not easy to learn, and even harder to apply, at times. The following story shows how the Lord has done what He promised in Karen's life, and made her paths straight.

Karen wanted to go to Bible School after graduating from high school, but because her dad became disabled, she went to work waiting tables, in order to help buy groceries for her parents. She was engaged to a young man named Steve, from her church in Billings. Steve was serving his country in Vietnam.

In November, Karen and Steve met in Hawaii, while he was on R & R. When she got off the plane, Karen immediately knew that Steve was not the man God planned for her to spend her life with. The realization of this could have caused Karen to spin out of control, but it didn't. She spent the next five days in Hawaii, having a really good time, but knowing that when she returned home, she needed to start dating again.

For four months prior to this time, two men, John and Gary, had been coming in the restaurant, flirting with Karen and asking her out. All that time, she had refused because she was engaged to Steve.

Then, right after Christmas, Gary came into the restaurant and asked her to go out to dinner with him. Karen wasn't really keen on that, so instead they went roller skating with a group of people that she worked with, on Friday night. The next morning, John came in and asked her to go out with him, and they made a date for that very night.

The first time John and Karen kissed, she heard bells, which scared her so she talked to her Pastor. He advised her to wait for Steve to return. After all, he was a Christian young man, but that was not the path God had laid out for Karen's life. Then a short time later, John asked Karen to marry him. Karen took a few days to consider; but her answer was 'yes'!

As it got close to the time for Karen and John to be married, Karen learned that she needed her birth certificate. Her parents kept a box of important papers in a closet, and Karen knew she would find it there. However, when she looked at it, she noticed that it was for 'Karen Louise Young', not for 'Karen Louise Selle'. She went back to the box and discovered another birth certificate, for Karen Louise Selle. Other than the last names, and the names of the parents, the birth certificates were identical.

When she questioned her parents, she learned that her mother had previously been married to another man, her biological father. When Karen's mother, Betty, was pregnant with her, she learned that her husband was unfaithful. Betty divorced this man, and later married Orville Selle, who eventually adopted Karen.

This news could have caused Karen to spin out of control, but she was following the path God had laid out for her.

Another trait in Karen is that she seems to always be in the right place, at the right time, to serve God and use the gifts and abilities He has given her. Her husband, John, can also attest to the fact that being in the right place, at the right time, is very important. John loves the out-of-doors and all it has to offer.

One day, John and his friend went duck hunting. In Montana, there are two different flyways: the Pacific flyway and the Central flyway. For years, the seasons and limits for these flyways were different. In fact, at times the duck season in the Central flyway might be open, while the Pacific flyway is closed. There is no line on the ground, no sign on a fence post, and really, no sure way to know which flyway a person is in.

John and his friend had crossed over the line between the two flyways without knowing it. They were in the right place to find ducks, and they were on public land, so they did not need permission to hunt. When they spotted some ducks on a reservoir, John shot two. Later in the day, when John returned home, the game warden was sitting in front of his house, waiting for him. Someone had seen John shoot these ducks and had turned him in, giving the license number of John's pickup. The fine for shooting these ducks was $27.50, which John and his friend split.

Even though he was in the right place to find ducks, he was in the wrong place for shooting those ducks. That Sunday, his Pastor spoke on the importance of being in the right place, at the right time, to serve God. In the bulletin, that Sunday, their Pastor made reference to the fact that $27.50 was a lot to pay for a duck. Only John, Karen, and John's friend knew what that reference was all about.

With God, to be in the right place, at the right time, requires a willingness to follow Him wherever he leads, as well as a willingness to use the gifts that He has given you. In addition to using the spiritual gifts God gave you, you must be willing to share what He has taught you, when He brought you through the difficult times you experienced.

God expects the believer to do good works for Him. He says in Ephesians 2:10, "For we are God's workmanship, created in Christ Jesus to do good works, which God prepared in advance for us to do". We are to be His instruments for touching hearts and changing lives. This requires that we seek God's will, not our own will, in every situation.

After John and Karen first moved to Helena, Montana, she felt that God was telling her, "Now it's time to concentrate on your kids." She became a member of the school board and served for two terms. During her time on the school board, plans were underway for a program to help children deal with abuse. Several people spoke against having this type of program in school.

They thought abuse was a topic to be discussed in the home. As Christian parents, it was their right to teach their children; it had no place in the school. The problem is that even though most parents would agree with this, few really sit down with their children and talk to them about such things.

After listening to those people, Karen stood up, crying, and said, "You know, I was abused as a little girl. If I had been told that I wasn't the guilty one then, I would be even healthier now. I think we need to let these kids know, from day one, if we teach them nothing else, it's not their fault." The motion passed and the new program was implemented. The next month after the program was introduced; two little children came forward, needing help to deal with what they'd been through. Karen was there on the school board, at the right time, and in the right place.

Carroll College, in Helena, has a host program for female soccer players. These young women are away from home, to attend this college, and need host families. When Karen and John were asked to serve as host parents one year, they gladly agreed. Their instructions were to attend a soccer game, once in a while, and just "be there" for the girls.

Their first host student was Becky. Just after this girl arrived, her boyfriend was injured while bow hunting in Colorado. He was in a tree stand, lost his balance and fell, breaking his neck. Karen was at a Bible study, when she received the call, and immediately left to be with Becky.

Karen picked her up at school and took her home for the night.

Becky won the Father Peoples award, an award given to the most inspirational player. It had been started with money that Father Peoples had given as a supporter of the program. On Sunday, Becky was given the Father Peoples award, then on Monday morning Father Peoples didn't wake up. He had died of natural causes. Karen was called again, and Becky spent the night with her and John.

When Becky graduated, her mom wrote Karen and John a letter of gratitude, telling them how much of a difference they had made in Becky's life, because they were there for her when she needed somebody. Karen and John had been in the right place, at the right time.

Karen is the secretary at a school in an under-privileged area of Helena, where the poverty rate is just over fifty percent. This gives Karen many opportunities to touch lives.

One mother of three children was in the school often, for Special Education meetings. She stopped by Karen's office one day, just to talk. As she turned to leave, Karen said to her, "I just want you to know that I love you." She whirled around and looked at Karen, as if she had slapped her. Then she said, "What did you say?" Karen repeated, "I love you."

Her response was, "Nobody has ever told me that in my life, unless they wanted sex." Karen started to cry, she went around the wall and gave her a big hug, saying, "Well, I want you to know that I really love you, and I'm here for you, if you need me."

Far too many times, Christians fail, when it comes to sharing the love of Jesus with their neighbors. We do not tell them that we love them, and we do not show them that we love them. The world is full of people who have never heard someone say, 'I love you', without expecting something in return.

Unfortunately, later on this woman's youngest daughter was molested. This little girl had her mom cut her hair really short and she started wearing her brother's clothes. She didn't want to be a girl anymore, because those bad things happen to little girls.

Because of Karen's background, God enabled her to talk with this beautiful little girl, and help her to deal with this terrible experience. On the day she had her first girl sleepover, she called Karen at school. She said "Mrs. Lorenz, I'm having girlfriends over tonight, and they're going to spend the night with me. I have girlfriends! You were right, I can be a girl. It's okay to be a girl." Again, Karen had been in the right place, at the right time; she was used by God to touch someone's heart.

Karen's older brother, Kenny, had two children, a boy and a girl. Travis, the son, was raised mostly by his mom. He became a kind of 'forgotten' child because his mother favored her daughter. In fact, he was a year old before he even rolled over. His physical needs were met, he was fed, clothed and cleaned, but he didn't receive much interaction.

The first time that John and Karen met Travis, he just climbed into their hearts, and they had a special bond from that day on. They always sent him a Christmas present and other little things throughout the year. When Travis joined the army, Kenny called Karen to tell her. From that very first day on, she wrote to him.

When Travis went to Iraq, Karen e-mailed him six days a week and the seventh day she would write him a paper letter. Travis received mail only once a week while he was in Iraq, so this way he received word from her each and every day. Through all that they developed quite a relationship and became very close.

On his second tour to Iraq, Travis was on duty on top of a police station in Baghdad. One of the other soldiers posted there wanted to move and asked Travis if he would trade

Divine Appointments

places with her. He agreed, and as they started, their movement alerted the enemy. Travis was shot and killed instantly.

When John and Karen received the call about Travis, they left immediately for Rochester, Minnesota. The first thing on the agenda was to plan the service, and Karen and John were very helpful. They picked out the music, as well as the scriptures to be used in the service. Travis was the first soldier from Minnesota killed in Iraq; and politics played big part in the service.

Travis's girlfriend reached out to Karen for comfort, and Karen had a chance to minister to her. This girl really needed someone to be there to listen, and not judge. Too many times, Christians make judgmental comments, instead of just listening and loving. People come to Jesus, because of the love that is shown to them, not because of someone telling them they are living wrongly!

Each time, Karen and John end up in the right place, at the right time, to be used by God to touch hearts, in a real and personal way. The secret to their lives is that, before doing anything, they bring it before the Lord, asking Him to guide and direct their lives. Karen has thought of retiring, but each time she does, God shows her that she is still needed right where she is.

Karen would also say that God is not fair, but He is more than fair. In fact they would say that God is their Guiding Light, their Rock in the time of storm, and their Salvation!

Things to Ponder

1. Do you see the Lord's handprint in your daily life and if so how?
2. Have there been times when you found your life spinning out of control? How could you have handled those times better?
3. How do you feel about the statement "God expects the believer to do good works for Him"?
4. The world is full of people who have never heard someone say, 'I love you', without expecting something in return. Is this something believers can change and if so how?
5. Karen and John end up in the right place, at the right time by asking God to guide and direct their lives. Is this something that all believers should incorporate into their lives?

10

In The Name of Jesus, Live!

When we accept Jesus as Lord and Savior, scripture says that we pass from death to life. John 5:24 says "I tell you the truth, whoever hears my word and believes him who sent me has eternal life and will not be condemned; he has crossed over from death to life". This refers to a spiritual death and life. Our life is no longer the same; it has changed.

At the end of the movie, Second Hand Lions, Walter makes a statement about his uncles that has stuck in my mind. He said that his uncles 'really lived.' The one thing that I want people to say about me, when I am gone, is that I really lived for Jesus. I have known a few people that I could honestly say really lived for the Lord.

In the New Testament, we read about Jesus bringing people, who had died physically, back to life. But, does He still do it today? For years, I would have told you 'no', but then I met a young man named Andrew Christofferson in Helena, Montana. Andrew has experienced a passing from death to life, in both a spiritual sense as well as a physical sense. He is one of those few people that I believe really lives for Jesus. The following shows a small portion of his life, in his quest to follow Jesus:

When Andrew was 18, he enrolled in a two year program at the Master's Commission ministry training school, part of the Assemblies of God Church. One commitment the students there make is, 'Any country, any time, God send us; God use us for Your glory, for what You want to do.' Andrew's group began to pray about going on an overseas mission trip, asking the Lord to show them where He wanted them to go. Through seeking the Lord's Will, they chose to go to Guatemala, where they were to work with 'Youth With A Mission' (YWAM).

They planned to go to several villages that were far into the jungle, and therefore mostly unreached, with the Word of

God. Because there were few roads into this area, they were required to backpack into these villages. To prepare, they began physical training and started out each morning with two hours from 7:00 to 9:00 am, and they ended each day with more training, from 7:00 to 8:30 pm.

A former Marine drill sergeant, their physical trainer, really put them through their paces. They trained with backpacks, loaded with about sixty pounds on their backs, while doing their exercises. They even learned to climb ropes with these backpacks on. In the end, they knew that they would be ready to pack into the mountains of Guatemala. During this time, they also held fund raisers, to help pay for their mission trip.

Finally the day arrived in April, 2004; they boarded their plane and began their flight to Guatemala. It was dark and raining, when they arrived in Guatemala City. Guards who looked to be no more than 18 years old, moved around the airport armed with machine guns. It definitely had the feel of a third world country – a very different experience for a young Montana man. Soon, they were picked up by the YWAM staff, and taken to their base, where they spent the night. Before heading for a much needed sleep, they loaded their backpacks, and found that they were much heavier than

In The Name Of Jesus, Live!

expected. The men's backpacks weighed between 80 and 90 pounds.

Eager to begin, these eleven young people piled into a Volkswagen bus at 3:00 A.M., and headed out on their adventure of a lifetime. The bus was over-crowded with the passengers and their gear, but the six hour trip seemed to fly by. When they reach the trailhead, the excitement was felt by everyone!

Soon they had unloaded their vehicle, taken a quick group photo, and were headed into the back country of Guatemala. Although they had spent a lot of time and energy preparing for this trip, by hiking around the mountains of western Montana, they soon found that they were really not prepared. The humidity was about 85 to 90 percent, the heat was more than they were used to, and mountains were much steeper, rising very quickly.

It seemed very desolate to Andrew as they started out, but as they moved further into the bush the scenery began to change. At one point, they came across two rope bridges, like what you would see in an Indiana Jones movie. These were quite long, and as Andrew stood in the middle of one, with the river underneath, he thought to himself, "I feel like I'm in a movie." This was not like anything he had experienced before, and it was just the beginning. In just a few days, Andrew would experience something that few people ever experience in their lives.

They reached the top of the mountain and headed into the valley below, on a very narrow trail. Each step had to be taken with considerable care. Because they were becoming dehydrated, their walking was made even harder. One wrong step could lead to disaster.

They were going to the little village of Chappelle. About a month before this trip, their leader, Dan, had made a scouting trip into the area, to check it all out. He found that there was a little church building in Chappelle that the Nazarenes had built in the 1960s. The villagers still used it for their meetings. Dan also learned that a Christian pastor traveled between the friendly villages, conducting services every second month. Dan informed the residents of Chappelle, that he and his team would arrive in one month, and asked that they be ready for them.

Several villagers saw the team coming, ran about two miles up the mountain, and offered to carry the team's backpacks. A young Guatemalan woman, who was no more than five feet tall, without shoes, motioned to one of the men to let her carry his backpack. At first he refused, but she insisted;

then she took it, placing it on her head as she raced down the trail!

They had hiked for two days, when the team reached the village of Chappelle. The village was made up of mostly mud huts, with a cement church building. That night, they had their first service in that old church. They sang spiritual songs, and Dan, their leader, shared the gospel message, and explained what the team planned to do there. This message was delivered through a translator, since Dan didn't speak Spanish.

The team found that, even though some of these people had accepted Jesus as their Lord and Savior, they had mixed the gospel with their former beliefs. This happens too often, in Christianity, when people are led to Jesus, but not discipled. It is easy to have wrong theology, when a person is not trained or discipled, in becoming a Christian or follower of Jesus. This had happened in Chappelle, and the team needed to work on teaching these believers about following Jesus.

On the third morning, Dan shared that he felt led of the Lord, to take a small group of the team, to some other villages in the area. This would mean that the rest would to stay behind, at Chappelle, to disciple the villagers, with the help of their interpreter. There would be three men going, which left one man and seven women, to continue the work in this village. The ones chosen to go with Dan, to these other villages were Andrew and his best friend Jason.

That evening the team asked some of the villagers, if they would come with them, to translate, and help share the gospel, with some other villages. There were, at the time, about five villagers who were strong in the Lord, so the team was sure that they would be willing to help share the gospel. The response was not what the team had expected, or wanted. Each one of them refused.

These villages were both hostile to the Gospel, and hostile to outsiders, which brought fear to the hearts of the five Christians from Chappelle. This is something that happens often in the church. Believers become afraid, and give into that fear, instead of doing what the Lord has called them to do.

Jesus tells us, in Luke 12:4-5, "I tell you, my friends, do not be afraid of those who kill the body and after that can do no more. But I will show you whom you should fear: Fear him who, after the killing of the body, has power to throw you into hell". The believer should never be afraid to do the will of the Lord. After all, if God is for us, who can be against us?

In The Name Of Jesus, Live!

Even though there were some good things happening in Chappelle, the team felt a strong calling of the Lord, to go to the people of these other villages, who needed to hear the Gospel. The next morning, the three men prepared to leave on this journey, without translators.

Although Andrew had asked Jesus into his heart when he was a very young boy, until about a year earlier, he was not really committed to following Him, wherever He would lead. One day, Andrew felt that God said to him, "It's either you follow Me, or you follow yourself." This was the point when Andrew was finally ready to follow the Lord, no matter where He would lead.

Before Andrew left, he wrote a letter to his family, telling them the plans of the team. In it, he told them, they were about to go to these villages to share the Gospel. If he did not come back, his family needed to know how important this was to him. He told them that believers need to be willing to lay down their lives for the Gospel, and that was just what he was willing to do, if necessary. Andrew finished his letter and gave it to one of his teammates, to give to his family, if he did not return.

For those of us living in the United States, life can be quite easy. Most of us have not only what we need, but also much of what we want, as well. The writers of the New Testament, lived during a time when, to be a Christian, was a life or death matter. To believers, living in countries where Christians are persecuted, it is a matter of life and death. However, that's not how it is for most of us in the free world. We have the freedom to worship any way we want. Until the Gospel becomes a life or death matter, it does not take on the same meaning for most of us who call ourselves Christians.

For Andrew, writing that letter to his family was the moment that he laid his life on the line for Jesus. From that point on, he knew that he would follow Jesus for the rest of his life. It didn't matter what happened to him; what mattered was the Gospel. There is great freedom in knowing that nothing else matters, except for Jesus, and telling others about Him.

The eleven team members took communion, at the rope bridge leading into Chappelle, before the three men headed out. They started climbing a very steep mountain, with the temperature about 100 degrees Fahrenheit. Even though, they were in the best physical condition of their lives, the climb was strenuous. Their goal was to reach some villages on a mountain, about twenty miles away.

In The Name Of Jesus, Live!

At the peak of the first mountain, they came across a family living in a mud hut. They also encountered a pack of wild dogs, which the family chased away. These dogs were very aggressive, so Andrew and his companions were glad, when they were chased away. Jason spoke a small amount of Spanish; he told this family what they were doing, and asked for the quickest way to get across the next valley, to the village they could see from the hut.

They had two options. They could go around the mountains on a road, but it was about a thirty mile trip. Or they could go down through the valley, which was about a ten mile hike. The team chose the shorter way. This family of twelve fed Andrew and his companions some tortillas, goat cheese and other things that they did not recognize. As they ate, they could feel the eyes of ten children staring at them; this made the team feel quite uneasy.

After finishing their meal, the three of them began their descent down the mountain. Had they known what was about to happen, they probably would have taken the longer, safer route. So many times, we as believers, take the safer route, intending to miss the areas of trouble ahead, but in doing so, we also miss out on seeing God perform a miracle!

Even though it was 6:00 pm, and would be dark in two to three hours, they left anyway, because they were excited to reach the next village and begin to share the Gospel. At first, the hike down the mountain was easy, but about halfway down things changed. The mountain became very steep, and Andrew found that he needed to hold onto tree branches, to lower himself down the terrain. As he slowly slid down the mountain, darkness began to set in. He stopped to put on his headlamp, and then continued the treacherous path.

As the group descended, Dan was in the lead, followed by Andrew; and Jason brought up the rear. About halfway down the mountain, Dan came to a rocky area, with a few small cliffs. He decided to go around, which brought him through a more heavily forested area. When Andrew reached this same spot, he made the decision not to go around, but to go right through it. This was a decision that would have far reaching effects on all three of them, for a long time to come!

Andrew could see a ledge about five feet in front of him, and another ledge about ten to twelve feet beyond it. He thought that he could just slide down to each one. As he started down he slipped on something, hit the first ledge, and fell head first to the next ledge, smashing into the ground.

Jason heard a scream like nothing he had ever heard before. He hurried down to the top of the cliff, looked over and saw Andrew in a crumpled heap at the bottom. He made his way around through the forest, as Dan came back up from below. They arrived at the same time. Both of these men were trained in first aid, and began to check Andrew for both breathing and a pulse. But soon it was clear, Andrew had neither.

While all this was taking place, Andrew was in the spirit; he knew that he was either dead, or very, very close to being dead. He felt an incredible peace, the kind of peace that comes only from God. The apostle Paul calls it a "peace that transcends all understanding" (Philippians 4:7).

As he stood there in the spirit, feeling that peace, he had an angel on his right, an angel on his left and an angel in front of him. These angels were between eight and ten feet tall; one might say that they were huge. At the same time, the presence of God was almost overwhelming, and even though Andrew could not see or touch Him, he just knew that God was there. Andrew became very excited; he was sure he was about to make a trip to heaven!

Meanwhile, Dan and Jason continued resuscitation efforts, but nothing worked. Dan moved off about ten feet from Andrew, to sit down on a rock and think, leaving Jason beside Andrew. The seriousness of the situation struck Jason, and he became very fearful. He knew there was no way to get help. They were in the jungle of Guatemala; without roads there was no way to get an ambulance. An airlift was also impossible. There was just nothing, humanly speaking, that they could do.

That previous year, they had studied about the power of God, and about the presence of God, in one's life. They had read and studied verses, like John 14:12, which says, "I tell you the truth, anyone who has faith in me will do what I have been doing. He will do even greater things than these, because I am going to the Father". They had also looked, in the book of Acts, at all the things that the Apostles did.

Yet, knowing all of this, they still felt defeated. Satan wants the believer to feel defeated, instead of believing the Word of God, and putting it into practice, because Satan thinks he has won. But Satan did not win here, and he doesn't have to win, in any of our lives!

After about a minute, Dan moved back to Andrew's limp body. Again, he checked for breathing and a pulse, but found neither. Dan didn't know what to do, but he determined that he could not take home a dead body. He took hold of Andrew's head and as he moved it back in line with Andrew's body, he prayed, "In the name of Jesus, live!" It was just a blur, as Andrew shot back into his body, and opened his eyes. One moment he was looking into the faces of angels; the next moment he was looking into the faces of Dan and Jason!

Five minutes had passed from the time Dan and Jason had first arrived to help Andrew; but now, they had new things to deal with. Andrew had a severe concussion, and since his heart started beating again, an artery near his elbow, sprayed blood all around. His left wrist and his right hand were also broken, and he had a few broken teeth, as well. They had to work quickly, to stop the blood loss, and prepare to get Andrew back up the mountain.

Around 10:30 pm, they started up the mountain, with Jason leading the way, and Dan behind Andrew, helping him along. The mountain was very steep, so these men had to literally pull themselves up the slope. This was difficult with Andrew's injuries, so at times, Dan had to push him up. Add to this, every few minutes, they had to stop, so Andrew could vomit. It was a very slow climb. At one point, Dan shook his head, and said to Andrew, "Man, God has something for you."

God Is Not Fair, He Is More Than Fair

They finally reached the top of the mountain. Jason pitched a tent, for Andrew and himself to stay in that night, and Dan left, heading back to Chappelle. From there, he would go out to get the truck, and try to drive around, to a road which came into that area. Jason kept watch over Andrew through the night, waking him up periodically, because of the concussion that Andrew had suffered.

They had come into contact with a dark, spiritual atmosphere in that place, so Jason spent a lot of time in prayer. He saw some small creatures running around, and felt a spirit of fear, like he had never felt before. He did not sleep at all, but just spent the night praying for the Lord's protection and touch. That morning, when Andrew awoke, he ran his tongue around his mouth, remembering the broken teeth. Instead of feeling broken teeth, he found that they were all in place!

Dan had reached the village, and sent the nurse in their team up to help Jason and Andrew. He then headed out to get their truck. Jason and the nurse prayed over Andrew, for his hands and other injuries, but nothing changed with his hands. Sometimes, God does a miracle, and sometimes He does not. The important thing is to always seek His will in our lives. After praying, they bandaged Andrew's hands, noting that both his wrist and hand were broken, and they were going to need to get him to the hospital, as quickly as possible. The rest of that day, they spent waiting for Dan, but remembering that when he left, he told them, it might take him three or four days, to hike out and return by road.

However, that evening around 5:00, Dan arrived with a few Guatemalan men to help. Soon they had Andrew loaded in the truck. Some of the men rode back, while the rest hiked back down the mountain to Chappelle. There were three of them in the front, with Andrew by the door, and four more in the back of a small Nissan pickup.

As they started out on a winding, dirt road, through the Guatemalan jungle, a light rain began to fall. Then, as they started to descend down the mountain, the clouds opened up and heavy rain poured down. The rain increased, turning the dirt to mud, and the road became very slippery. The truck slid to and fro; on the uneven path. They slid around the corners without guard rails, the truck moved up against the mountain and then back toward the cliff. At one point, Andrew looked down, and saw that the mountain dropped off a couple thousand feet. This would be enough to put fear into the heart of bravest person, which was shown, as the men in the back were ready to jump, at any moment! Then Andrew remembered what God had done the day before. God had brought him back to life, the day before; so surely, he was not going to die this day!

So often, when difficult things come into our lives, we give into fear, instead of remembering what God has done in the past, and trusting Him with the future. Satan would love to have all believers huddled in fear, because that makes the believer ineffective. This is a ploy used by terrorists and Satan alike, because Satan is the first terrorist there ever was!

The truck got stuck several times, and each time the men worked hard to get it out. Finally, they reached a paved road and made their way to a hospital, where staff took X-rays and placed Andrew's left wrist in a cast. The hospital staff also wanted to operate on his right hand, but Andrew opted to return to Helena for that.

Andrew was taken to a Pastor's house, and from there, to the WYAM base. He stayed there for two days, waiting to return to Montana. While there, he had time to reflect on what had happened to him. He told Dan about seeing the angels, and feeling the presence of God like he never had before.

Dan shared with Andrew how he had prayed over him, and watched him come back to life! This experienced caused Andrew to really marvel at God's purpose.

In The Name Of Jesus, Live!

Later, Andrew prayed, asking God why he had lived. He was sure that given the circumstances, he should be dead. The Lord responded that he had more things for Andrew to do.

Andrew's defining moment was when he prayed, "Whatever happens, I'm in your safety, and if I die, I die." I know, without a doubt, that Andrew agrees with me: "God is not fair, He is more than fair!" Andrew should have died on that Guatemalan mountain that day. He WAS dead; but because of God, he is alive, both physically and spiritually! Andrew truly is Alive in Christ.

Things to Ponder

1. Have you ever known someone that you could honestly say really lived for the Lord?
2. Andrew finally reached the point where he was ready to follow the Lord, no matter where He would lead. Have you reached that point in your life?
3. Does Jesus still do miracles like He did when He was here on the earth? Have you heard of any similar stories?
4. "Sometimes, God does a miracle, and sometimes He does not. The important thing is to always seek His will in our lives." How do you feel about that statement?
5. "So often, when difficult things come into our lives, we give into fear." How have you been able to overcome that fear?

11

Meanwhile Back at Chappelle

What is the Will of God? Jesus said it best, when He was asked, "What is the greatest commandment?" He answered: "Love the Lord your God with all your heart, and with all your soul, and with all your strength, and with all your mind, and love your neighbor as yourself". (Luke 10:27) He also said, "Go and make disciples of all nations, baptizing them in the name of the Father and of the Son and of the Holy Spirit, and teaching them to obey everything I have commanded you". (Matt 28:19-20) The Will of God is that we love Him and that we love our neighbors, teaching them to follow Him. This was just what the whole team wanted to do!

When Dan, Andrew, and Jason left, the team's goal was to continue doing ministry, so they split up, with the women on the team sharing with the women of the village and the remaining man sharing with the men. They spent time reading through the Bible, because most of the natives had never even seen a Bible, much less, read from one.

Even before Dan, Andrew, and Jason left Chappelle, the Lord was at work, preparing for the things that were about to take place. In Isaiah 45:2, the Lord says: "I will go before you and will level the mountains; I will break down gates of bronze and cut through bars of iron". This means that God will go ahead of us, removing all the obstacles that would hinder believers from accomplishing His Will. He was preparing not just Dan, Andrew, and Jason for what would happen with them, but He was also preparing the way for the work the rest of the team would be doing in Chappelle.

The night before Dan, Andrew, and Jason left, the women of the team were in the big mud hut they shared. God was beginning to move. In the middle of the night, one of the leaders of the women started tapping Lindsay Dick on her back. Lindsay, who now lives in Harlowton, Montana, rolled over to see what she wanted. Lindsay thought this woman was awake, but saw that she was still sleeping. Then this

Meanwhile Back At Chappelle

leader began to speak words of prophesy about some of the team members. She prophesied about each person individually; then prayed for them, all the time remaining asleep.

After each prayer, Lindsay rolled over and tried to go back to sleep, only to be awakened again by the tapping. This happened four or five times that night, with the last one being about Jason. Some very strong things were prophesied about Jason, including that he wasn't strong enough and it was going to be very hard for him. Then this woman laid back down, facing Lindsay, and in her sleep, she told Lindsay to pray for Jason. Each time before, this woman had prayed.

After the first time Lindsay was awakened, she wrote down everything that was happening, to help her remember. As she prayed for Jason, with everyone else in the hut asleep, she felt a little strange, knowing that something was going to happen the next day. Yet, at the same time, she was encouraged, knowing that God was in control and He would work everything out, in His perfect way.

Lindsay was awakened one more time. But this time the woman, in her sleep, began to preach a message to the valley where they were, in perfect Spanish. Although this woman and Lindsay knew some Spanish, the message was in perfect

Spanish, and amazingly, Lindsay understood it completely! In this message, this woman spoke about the fact that darkness and light cannot be married. Again taking up her notebook, Lindsey wrote down every word the woman spoke in Spanish that night. At last, she was able to go to sleep.

The next morning, it was decided that Dan, Andrew and Jason were going to go on to the next village. The rest would stay in Chappelle, to minister to the villagers there. Lindsay had not told anyone about what had happened the night before. She kept it to herself, until that afternoon. When she finally was able to speak to the woman who had awakened her the previous night, Lindsay asked her if she knew what she had done.

This woman responded that she had several dreams in which she was talking to Lindsay. She felt like God was speaking through her, and that at one point, she was preaching to this valley. Lindsay then told her that she had actually done just that, and that Lindsay had written it all down. These two were then the only ones who knew something was not right, and there was difficulty ahead, for the team.

All of this was overwhelming. Lindsey couldn't understand why all this had happened, or what she was supposed to do with it. If she tried to tell someone, would they believe her, or would they think she was crazy? She just kept mulling it over in her mind, trying to gain some kind of understanding of it.

Through the whole day, Lindsay could feel a spiritual heaviness around her, she and the rest of the team, spent their free time worshiping, and praying to the Lord. At one point, she was on the back side of their mud hut, facing the mountain that Dan, Andrew and Jason were climbing up, playing her guitar and worshiping the Lord.

Another lady from the team was singing, when the Lord started speaking to Lindsay's heart. He reassured her that He had the three men in His Hands, and He would take care of them. At that same time, the other lady sang, "You have them in your hands, Lord." God has His own way of telling us just to trust in Him; for He, and He alone, is in control. Lindsay was comforted in knowing that everything was going to be alright, and she was not to worry.

It is so hard not to worry, when we know in our heart, that something terrible is about to happen. This becomes our point of focus, because it is hard to focus on God, when things seem to be going wrong around us. The demonic forces work very hard, to take the believer's focus away from God, and place it on the things around us, because doing so makes us ineffective. We need to try <u>not</u> to focus on the problem, but focus on the only One Who has a solution to the problem — the Lord God!

That night, the women started to retire, but all of them were restless and nervous, unable to get to sleep. They decided to go outside and light a fire. They sat around it talking, and as one shared some of her life experiences, they saw a light on the mountain. They were confident that it was a headlamp flashing, and thought the three men were signaling the team that they were alright.

At first, the team members in Chappelle were overjoyed that everything was okay; but that joy turned to fear, as the light continued to flash. They came to the realization that the light was flashing because it was passing behind trees. Also, they noticed that the light was moving at a much faster speed than a person could move. So their minds were filled with all kinds of questions, which they expressed to each other. They came to the conclusion that it was either an angel, or one of their guys with a headlamp. But all of them had headlamps, so there should be three lights!

A feeling of panic came over them, as they realized something was terribly wrong, and they could do nothing about it. Then, the strength of the Lord came upon them, and they started to pray! When the evil one brings difficult circumstances into the believer's life, he is trying to take our focus off of God; but a perfect response to that is to pray, seeking God's Will.

As they prayed, they began to form a plan: Lindsay, as well as the women's leader, who kept waking Lindsay the night before, and the male nurse, started down from the hut, to the point where the path down the mountain came into the village. Lindsay carried a five gallon water jug, the nurse brought his medical supplies, and the leader came along for support. The rest of the team stayed at the hut watching, waiting and praying. The Lord often calls the believer to watch, wait, and pray, even though it is difficult to be still, and just trust Him for the outcome.

The three of them ran down the hill, with water and supplies, to meet whoever was coming down the mountain, knowing that something was very wrong. They arrived at the bridge, which crossed the river at the edge of the village, just as Dan came across it. He was alone, so these three knew for sure, that something had happened.

In the eyes of Lindsay and the team, Dan was the strongest man they had ever met. He was not just strong physically, but also emotionally; he was seldom moved by anything. He was their fearless leader, extremely strong in the Lord, and they believed that he could do just about anything.

When he got across the bridge, Dan fell onto his knees and started to cry. This behavior could easily have caused a weaker believer to fall away. Many times, a person bases his belief system solely on the faith he sees in his leader. The believer needs to be careful to remember, that we are all just people, and we are not perfect. No matter how good a leader may be, sooner or later, he may let us down. The leader may have come to the end of his strength, and we need to lend our strength to him. We are to help each other, and trust the Lord to lead us all.

This thought hit Lindsay: Either Dan was trying to teach them how to deal with tragic situations, or this was something really, really bad! He had told them when he left, that he would not come back without Andrew and Jason. But there he was, by himself. He just kept crying and crying, saying, "I'm so sorry, I'm so sorry!" He was all scratched up, and Lindsay could tell that he was scared beyond words!

Dan was carrying a big stick, and he finally began talking about the wild dogs. Later, they found out that those wild dogs had attacked him, after he had left Andrew and

Meanwhile Back At Chappelle

Jason. During this ordeal, Dan heard a voice speaking to his mind, saying, "I'm going to kill you, I'm going to kill the rest of your team, and you're all dead!" The voice was trying to make him give up. He fought against the dogs with all his might, and could feel himself losing. Then suddenly, a bright light appeared behind him, and a voice said, "This is My child and you are to leave him alone!" The dogs let go and backed off, letting Dan get up, and continue down the mountain.

Dan had taken a GPS reading at the place where he left Andrew and Jason. He then left all his water with them and began running down the mountain. When the team below saw his light coming down the mountain so fast, it appeared to them that an angel must be carrying him. That is a possibility; but we don't know.

They were at the river, with Dan kneeling, sobbing, and saying "I'm so sorry, I'm so sorry!" Soon Dan added that Jason couldn't make it. Because he didn't say anything else, they thought that something had happened to Jason. But in Dan's confusion, he was trying to tell them that Jason was still with Andrew, and he wasn't coming down.

Dan was confused, and severely affected by dehydration; the nurse started an IV on him. Then they began to walk back up to the mud hut, planning to meet with the rest of the team, and figure out what to do next. Dan was very afraid of the dogs in the village, so Lindsay had to go in front of him, with a stick to chase away any dogs. Dan was a former body builder and a power lifter, but because of the extreme exhaustion, the attack of the wild dogs, and the spiritual torment he had been through, he was reduced to fear of those dogs.

The valley they were in was known for its spiritual darkness, and that night it was really coming out. Lindsay still remembers that some nights, she could feel the evil, even before any of this took place. At times, human sacrifice took place, as the powers of darkness seemed to claim the area as their own.

When the team arrived back at the mud hut, some hovered around Dan getting him food to eat and more water to drink. The rest of the team gathered together in prayer for Dan, Andrew and Jason, not knowing for sure even what to pray about, because they still did not know what had happened to Andrew and Jason. They waited for Dan to reveal what had happened, praying through the night.

After three or four hours of Dan crying, and saying that Jason couldn't make it, he finally told them that Andrew had fallen and broken his neck, but he did not tell them that God had healed him. In shock, the team members began to question Dan about the whereabouts of Andrew and Jason. Then, after quite a while had passed, Dan told them that God had healed Andrew, he was okay, and Dan had a plan to get them out. Even in our weakest moment, God has a plan and will work it out through us, if we are just willing to trust Him with the outcome.

Early in the morning, Dan, and two members of the team, left the village, planning to go to one of the cities. During a previous trip, Dan had scouted out where the team would spend their time in ministry. Now he remembered being very close to the place he had left Andrew and Jason. Knowing this helped the rest of the team members see God's hand in the situation.

At the same time, the male nurse headed up the mountain, to minister to Andrew and Jason. The plan was for everyone to meet together, at the place Dan had left Andrew and Jason, and then to transport Andrew out in a pickup, to get medical help. They would also help Jason to deal with the spiritual aspects of what he had experienced that night.

That left a smaller number of the team to carry on with ministry in the village. There had been just two who spoke some Spanish, but one of them went to help with Andrew, leaving Lindsay as the only one to interpret, as the team continued to do ministry. Everything would be fine, because Lindsay was, and still is, a strong believer in Jesus.

The Scripture says, in 1 Peter 4:11, "If anyone serves, he should do it with the strength God provides, so that in all things God may be praised through Jesus Christ". God had called Lindsay and the others to serve on this mission team, and they were only able to do it through the strength that comes from the Lord. They put their trust in God, saying, "Okay, we're here, we'll do it, and we'll figure it out."

While the others were gone, the ones who remained kept doing what they were called to do; they went from hut to hut, speaking with the villagers and praying for them, in spite of their limited language skills. That night, everyone was to come together, to hear a message from God given by one of the other members. Lindsay was to translate it into Spanish for the villagers the best she could, even though her Spanish was limited, and she did not know many of the words she might need.

Lindsay had not yet shared with the rest of the team, about what had happened in the middle of the night, because it still did not make a lot of sense to her, but she was about to understand. One of the team members got up to speak, and began sharing a message of how darkness and light cannot be joined together; that is, they cannot be married. This was the exact same message that her leader had spoken to her the night before, in Spanish, while the leader was asleep.

Lindsay knew for sure that the message the team member gave to the villagers was from God, because it was confirmed by what had transpired the night before. She prayed, "Wow, Lord, I don't know all you're doing, but You're pretty amazing!"

This was God's message for this valley: They could not stay in darkness, if they were going to follow Jesus. These villagers had allowed a lot of witchcraft, and other things, into their walk with Jesus, and this had to be removed from their lives. As believers and followers of God, we must be careful not to bring anything extra into our relationship with Jesus. We need to be careful also, how we interpret the Bible, so that we really understand God's purpose for us.

The next day, brought a very big rain storm, and the team members were concerned about what they should do. They did not know yet, how things were coming with getting Andrew out. As the rain poured down, they went out of their hut, and had a time of worshiping the Lord. There they were, dancing and worshiping God in the rain, because they felt such a need to be joyful! They had no idea what was happening with Andrew, Dan and Jason.

Still, they kept doing what they had come to do. Ministering where they could, and listening to God. Finally, one of the team members returned and told them that Andrew was flying home to Montana. More of the team members returned, and they continued doing ministry in the village, for a few more days. Then, they all went back to the YWAM base, in Guatemala City, and from there, they all flew back home. Andrew met them at the airport, in Helena, with casts on both of his arms. It was a very exciting, crazy time!

Lindsay had not seen Andrew fall, but she was part of all the things leading up to his fall, and what happened after it. This was a totally different experience than she had expected to have, in Guatemala, but it was a life changing experience, as well. Her faith in the living God took on a whole new meaning, for she had felt the hand of God in her life. He not only had raised Andrew from the dead, but He was also moving against the spiritual darkness in Chappelle, touching many lives.

After looking at the x-rays, the chiropractor asked Andrew if he had ever had a broken neck, because necks do not look like this, unless they have been broken. That was a confirmation to Andrew that what he had gone through, had actually happened! There are many times, in the life of the believer, when he questions himself, as to whether something really took place. That is where faith is strengthened.

Lindsay's husband, Bryce, is a youth pastor in Harlowton, Montana, and Andrew is a youth pastor, in Helena, Montana. During the summer of 2012, Bryce and Lindsay, along with Andrew and Danielle, Andrew's wife, took their youth groups on a mission trip to Guatemala. Although they did not go back to the village of Chappelle, just returning to Guatemala would be quite an experience, as they waited to see just what God would have in store for them on this trip!

Looking back at Lindsay and Andrew's experience, I have to say, again, God is not fair, He is more than fair. He constantly does amazing things in the lives of believers. Lindsay and Andrew would both agree.

Things to Ponder

1. "God will go ahead of us, removing all the obstacles that would hinder believers from accomplishing His Will." Knowing this, believers should be ready to step out to do the will of God, but many times we hold back. Why?
2. Lindsey held back on sharing what the Lord had revealed to her while her leader slept. Is there a time to tell and a time to remain quite?
3. "The demonic forces work very hard, to take the believer's focus away from God, and place it on the things around us, because doing so makes us ineffective." How can the believer overcome this?
4. Lindsay still remembers that some nights, she could feel the evil in that valley. Have you ever been in a place that you could feel the evil around you?
5. "As believers and followers of God, we must be careful not to bring anything extra into our relationship with Jesus." What are some things that believers bring into their relationship with Jesus?

12

God's Way

I just watched a YouTube video on church fights. A Pastor, who was appointed by his Bishop, returned to find that the trustees had changed the locks on the church, and he could not get in. In this video, the pastor was having a heated discussion with a lady, when she slapped his face. He in turn punched her, knocking her to the ground! From there, the fight escalated to a total mess! Neither person acted in a Christ-like manner; both were at fault. And, what the people saw, must have made many say, "I sure don't want to have anything to do with those crazy Christians!"

Several churches I have been involved with have been very set in their ways of doing things. It seemed to me that their theme song would be the chorus, 'I Shall Not Be Moved'. I believe that there are some things that we definitely should hold on to, including the authority of Scripture in the life of the church, as well as our belief that the Bible, in its original text, is without errors. But there are other things that the church clings to, that are really just individual preferences. So many times, the likes and dislikes of the people get in the way of reaching others for the Lord. When a church refuses to use whatever will reach others for Christ, it has failed to carry out the great commission. The church must always reach people where they are – not expect them to make the changes we think are necessary and find their way to us.

My friend, Larry Salway, Pastor of He Sapa New Life Church, in Rapid City, South Dakota, might be considered by some, as having a rather unconventional way of 'doing church.' He has the sanctuary set up in a semicircle, rather than rows of chairs all facing the front. The musical instruments at He Sapa New Life, are those of our Native American people.

Pastor Larry, and his wife, Dale, spent twenty years of ministry, in Arizona, with the Church of the Nazarene. He served as District Superintendent, for the Southwest Indian

District of the Nazarene, for seven years. Larry and Dale were also Church Planters there. Then, God laid it on their hearts to return to South Dakota, where Larry came from.

The Salways came back with the intention of Pastoring a Native American Church. At that time, there was only one Wesleyan Native American Church, in South Dakota, and that was in Rapid City. This Church consisted of one native couple, and the rest were white missionaries, who felt that Larry was "too Indian" in his ways. They thought his preaching was "too Indian" as well. Larry and Dale started rebuilding the work, by visiting people in their homes and at the hospital. By becoming part of their lives, the attendance began to grow.

Larry is a Lakota speaker, so he preaches in Lakota and translates into English. They began teaching the people some of the hymns in Lakota, and he prayed in Lakota and English. As people heard about what was happening, they began coming to the services. There were about 80 people coming, for a few months, and that increased to about 120. The Chapel was made to hold 80 people, so at 120, it felt crowded, and the attendance dropped. They tried to find a larger place to meet; and at one point, they met in an old horse barn.

About this time, the Wesleyan Native Ministries Board decided to sell the property where their church was located, as they had sold off all the other native Churches in South Dakota. Dr. Jerry Yellow Hawk, a retired Wesleyan Pastor, and former District Superintendent, along with six of the elderly people, came to Larry, with their concern about this new development. They asked Larry to go to Indiana and present their cause to Wesleyan Native Ministries Board. The property and land was valued at about 1.2 million dollars, because of its location, and the people just did not have the money to buy it.

The property was officially listed for sale, and Larry, Dale, and the people began to earnestly seek the Lord. They fasted and prayed, reminding God they needed the building as their place of worship. They prayed that no one else would even make a bid on the property, and no bids were placed at that time. Only after the bidding had closed, had one church group made an offer of three hundred thousand dollars, but it was too late, and the offer was refused.

Larry went to the board meeting with a bid of one dollar for a property valued at 1.2 million dollars! Surely, no one would accept that. The board decided to rent the property to Larry and his church; and set the rent to cover only the insurance and utilities for one year! At the end of that year, they would sell it for sure.

At the end of that year, Larry and Isaac Smith, the Dakota District Superintendent, went to the board meeting of the Wesleyan Native Ministries. They were at a loss as to what to do, but the Lakota people kept telling Larry that God had provided that building for them, and He was going to move on their behalf. Larry took with him a video he had made, showing the work that was being accomplished in his ministry. It showed baptisms, lots of people getting saved, the outreach that was being done, and the revivals that had taken place. Larry had condensed all this into a video that lasted about seven and a half minutes.

There they were, once more; meeting about the sale of the property. Larry again offered to buy it for the price of one dollar. He asked the board to watch his video before they made a decision. Then, he told the board that the faces of the people they saw were a result of what God had done, in the last six years, through the use of that property, and the prayers of His people. With that said, the board went into an executive session, so Larry and Isaac were asked to step outside.

The next few minutes, seemed like hours, as Larry and Isaac walked the halls, praying to the Lord for His Will to be done. Larry called his wife, and the people of the church, asking them to pray for the board to make the right decision, at the same time doubting the outcome. After all, who in their right mind would accept one dollar for a property worth 1.2 million dollars. Satan loves it, when the believer doubts the power of God in any situation, but God tells us to just trust in Him for the outcome.

When Larry and Isaac were called back into the meeting, they were informed that, after watching the video, the board decided it would gladly sell the property for one dollar! Now, that is the hand of God at work! Larry reached into his pocket, but found that he did not have any money with him at the time. So, he turned to Isaac, and said, "Isaac, let's begin a real good relationship. Pay it." Isaac said, "Buddy, you owe me." He got out a dollar, they shook hands, and cemented a relationship lasting for years to come!

The greatest joy, for Larry and the church, came about thirty days later, when a representative of Wesleyan Native Ministries Board came to the worship service, with the free and clear title to the property! Larry would tell you that this, for him, was the height of his ministry of 46 years, for God had intervened in what seemed like an impossible situation. Since that time a lot of money, effort, and elbow grease have been put into that property.

A short time later, Larry and Dale felt the need to video record their service, and use those videos as an outreach to even more of their people. They began to record their services with their little camcorder. They made copies, one at a time, for this outreach. At that time, they made and sent out about twenty DVDs each week.

One day, Isaac Smith asked Larry what he thought was his greatest need, in reaching the lost. Humbly, Larry told him that it sure would be nice if they had a better system for making those DVDs. Isaac let that need be known around the District, and Celebrate Church, in Sioux Falls, South Dakota, took that as a challenge. They purchased a system for over eight thousand dollars! That system is now being used to produce more than 230 DVDs each week, which are sent to households in seven states! What a blessing!

South Dakota alone has nine different reservations, and at this writing, Larry and Dale send DVDs into seven of them. Others are sent to reservations in Minnesota, Wyoming, Montana, Arizona and New Mexico. With these DVDs, the word of God is reaching over seven thousand people and

God has provided a way of reaching people in an unconventional way.

At one point, the Lord laid on Larry's and Dale's hearts a deep desire to reach the Lakota people, but no one has ever been able to make a Native American Church sustainable for the long haul. They cried out to the Lord, asking what they were doing wrong and pleading with Him to show them the way of reaching Larry's own people. The Lord spoke to his heart, as he read Matthew 28:18-20, which says,

> Then Jesus came to them and said, "All authority in heaven and on earth has been given to me. Therefore go and make disciples of all nations, baptizing them in the name of the Father and of the Son and of the Holy Spirit, and teaching them to obey everything I have commanded you. And surely I am with you always, to the very end of the age."

God was saying that the power comes from Him, that all the resources needed are in Christ, and it is the responsibility of the believer to take Jesus to the lost.

Before the Europeans came west, whenever a Chief, or some other important person, had a message for another tribe, he would take a gift to the elders of that tribe. He would offer that gift, knowing that the gift could be either accepted, or rejected. If the gift was rejected, the messenger would be asked to leave; but if the gift was accepted, the people were obligated to listen. This is proper protocol, and is something that had never been done before, by the church.

When the Native American people were placed on reservations, the church sent out ministers to establish Christianity on these reservations. The church built rectangular buildings, the ministers preached from the Word, with Bible in hand, and expected the people to come running. For around 250 years, this went on, with little or no success, and no one could figure out why. What needed to be done was to restore proper protocol.

That is just what Larry and Dale began to do, to reach Native American People. When they went into a community, they gave a gift to the elders. If the elders accepted the gift, Larry and Dale received the right to bring the Gospel to that community. Larry and Dale had learned that the important thing was to follow proper protocol. By doing so, they affirmed the culture. In doing so, they found the way God had provided for them, to reach their people.

Larry and Dale will never go into a community that has an already established evangelical work. They will resource them, help them, and even come alongside them, but they will never fight over territory. This is something that the church should always do. But, many times, people do a church plant instead, because their denomination is not represented in that community. I, personally, have had that happen to me, as I pastored a small church in a small community. The result was that there were then two even smaller churches, with even fewer resources.

In the summertime, Larry and Dale use volunteer teams to do work in a community. They fix porches, repair windows and doors, work on handicapped ramps that are beginning to fall apart, and anything else that needs repair. They expect nothing in return. This is a great way to gift people, and earn the right to share the Gospel. Sharing the labor of love is something that has been very successful, in meeting people, wherever they have been. The secret is to expect nothing in return, for we are working for the Lord, and not for man.

At every meeting they do, the Gospel of John is passed out to everyone attending. Each individual who gives their heart to Jesus receives a New Testament, which Larry and Dale call 'The Sacred Road Book'. That person is then registered to receive DVDs, making it possible for them to be discipled. At the end of six months of discipleship, they receive a full Bible, which is called 'The Words of Wisdom, from the Great One Above'. This is how Larry and Dale are able to successfully reach out into new communities. This would be considered unconventional, but people are being saved, and that is what matters!

A DVD ministry like this costs a lot of money — more than the average person can even imagine. Shortly after they had run out of money to send out the DVD's, Larry was at a meeting with a group of pastors. He was asked if there was something he needed, to carry on his ministry. Larry was very tempted to ask for money for the DVD ministry, but felt the Lord tell him that He knew the need, and He would provide. Instead, Larry replied that their greatest need was prayer, that God would move and melt the right hearts.

That same night, Larry and Dale were invited out to a dinner, which included a man from New York. This man wanted to invest in the ministry, at Pine Ridge, South Dakota, so Larry told him about the work there and also shared about the DVD ministry. This man returned to New York, and Larry thought that was the end of it. But, a short time later, he received a letter from this man.

Upon opening it, Larry found a check for $25,000, along with a letter, stating the check was for the DVD ministry! One of God's names, from the Old Testament, is Jehovah Jireh, which means God will provide. Had Larry asked those pastors for money, he would have missed out on seeing God provide, in an unconventional way, and this man would have missed out on a blessing as well!

In the weeks leading up to Christmas, Larry and Dale do an outreach, in several communities in South Dakota. In 2011, they prepared to go to Mission, South Dakota, which is on the Rosebud Reservation, intending to conduct an outreach, for the first time. They intended to gift the people who attended the meeting. They were prepared with Christmas gifts for the children, blankets for the elders, and a traditional Native American meal for everyone in attendance.

They had never done an outreach in Mission, so they took food for about 500 people, thinking that they had more than enough. Little did they know, what God had planned! As they saw the number of people coming, they prayed to God, asking Him to stretch the food, so that they would have enough. God did just like He did, when He fed the 5000! God made sure that everyone had plenty to eat, and all the children received a Christmas gift!

That day, seventy-eight, of the 750 people, gave their hearts to the Lord, starting a new life in Christ! That year, Larry and Dale also conducted outreaches in Pierre, Eagle Butte, White River, Marten, Cherry Creek, and Rapid City. A total of over 2100 people heard the Gospel story, and around 210 people gave their hearts to the Lord!

Larry has seen the hand of God in his life, for many years. He first heard about Jesus, at the age of six, when he was invited to attend Sunday School. He heard about his need for salvation, and that it comes only through a relationship with Jesus, but instead he returned to the traditional way, the medicine way and was a pipe carrier. He became really involved in that religion, but Jesus never gave up on him.

When he was nineteen, living in a tent in the dead of winter, a young white man came to shoot pheasants, grouse, deer, or rabbits, and left them at the entrance to Larry's tent. Larry had no money, nor food, and was in for a terrible winter. In fact, Larry would most likely have starved to death that winter, if it had not been for that young man, who brought him food about twice a week. Because of that kindness, this young man earned Larry's respect and admiration, in a big way. In June, when this young man invited Larry to go with him to a camp meeting, in Hot Springs, South

Dakota, Larry knew he just could not say no. This young man, without even knowing it, had restored proper protocol with Larry, by gifting him repeatedly.

The camp meeting was at Brainerd Indian School, which is run by the Wesleyan Church. Larry heard the same wonderful story of Jesus, that he had heard when he was six years old. Now he was nineteen, a medicine man trained in the old ways — the traditional ways. At this camp meeting, he heard time and time again, about the love of Jesus.

He heard that Jesus died for him, so that no matter what Larry had done in the past, he could be made right with God, by trusting in what Jesus had already done for him. He asked himself, how could that be? How could someone love him so much; could it even be possible? He finally surrendered, and gave his heart to Jesus! Jesus delivered him from all the things he was involved in, and set him free!

Tradition is not as important as touching the hearts of people for Jesus. This is best done by accepting people where they are, and letting God change their lives, as He sees fit. Believers, too many times, look at a situation, and say, "This is how we have always done it!" When it does not work, we cannot figure out why. But when God looks at people, He knows what will work the best, and He calls people to follow Him, in reaching those people.

As believers, we must put aside our traditions, look for where God is working, and join with Him, in sharing the Gospel. We must learn, that what has worked in the past, may not work now, so we must change, in order to reach people for Jesus.

Larry knew that he had deserved death, but now he knows, that, if a person will just give his heart to Jesus, anything is possible! He has seen God change people's lives from drug and alcohol addiction, literally at the bottom of the barrel, to being great and upright people of God, no longer in need of the crutch of alcohol or drugs.

Larry would agree that God is not fair, He is more than fair!

Things to Ponder

1. Is there a right way and a wrong way to have a Church service?
2. What kind of things can get in the way of reaching others for the Lord?
3. How can the protocol of gifting be applied to all nationalities in reaching others for Christ?
4. What should a group consider before doing a church plant in a community?
5. How do you feel about "accepting people where they are, and letting God change their lives"?

13

It Is All A Matter Of Focus

*A*ttitude is the one thing that shows, more clearly than anything else, a person's heart. It can be that sweet perfume that draws one person to another, or that strong smelling, foul odor that makes one person flee from another.

Compare, for instance, a sweet perfume, with skunk odor. When perfume is made, the fine scent that is made with oil will not last very long, if it is mixed with distilled water. In order to make that scent last, the manufacturer uses musk, from skunks!

It no longer smells like a skunk, so the people wearing it smell nice. That nice smelling fragrance actually draws people to each other, in turn, enhancing relationships.

Wearing a nice fragrance even makes us feel good about ourselves.

When a skunk sprays, the odor lasts for a very long time, and it's so bad that even the skunk can't stand it. Even when diluted, the smell is very strong, and will last for days.

Years ago, my wife and I owned a hardware store, in Hysham, Montana, which was built in the early 1900's. Under the floor, an open area ran clear to the back room. I opened the store at 7:30 am, and in the summer, I would open all the doors, to cool it off inside. I used an old paint can to prop open the front door.

One morning after I had opened, a customer entered through the front door and walked rather loudly down the aisle. After he made his purchase, he proceeded out the front door. He accidentally bumped the can, and the door slammed shut with a bang. Unknown to me, a skunk had entered through the back, and gone under the floor of the main part of the store. The slamming of the door frightened the skunk, causing him to spray his calling card under the floor.

Now, a skunk cannot even stand his own smell, so he left; but his calling card remained, making the store reek. There was nothing I could do to clean it up. The smell is impossible to cover up, so I had to keep the doors open, and tolerate the stinky environment the best I could.

Hysham is a very small town; so small that if a person got stuck in the mud outside of town, the news of that event would beat the person back to town! The news of what had happened carried quickly throughout the whole community, and for the next few days, business was very slow. People only came into the store if they absolutely had to, and stayed as short of a time as they could.

Another time, one of the men in town got sprayed in the face by a skunk. The odor is so strong from skunk spray that after a few seconds, this man could no longer smell anything, including himself. Sometime during the day, he went into the Post Office, which was a very small building, to get his mail. For several hours later, everyone who entered the Post Office was greeted by a very strong skunk odor. Again, word traveled quickly, and most of Hysham stayed home from getting their mail, but the post master was stuck there the whole day.

A person's attitude is just like that skunk musk. When a person has a good attitude, people are attracted; but when a person has a bad attitude, people are repelled. You might wonder how we can have and keep a good attitude, when everything around us goes wrong. I believe it is all a matter of focus. A person's attitude is a result of what that person focuses on.

If I focus on myself, my problems, and the things going wrong about me, I will have a bad attitude, driving people away. If I focus on Jesus in the midst of my problems, I will have a good attitude, with a sweet smelling aroma attracting people to Jesus. Satan works overtime, trying to take the believers' focus off of Jesus, and putting it on themselves. If he can accomplish that, he makes the believer ineffective.

Clark Pritchard is one person who has learned this valuable lesson, in his walk with the Lord. Instead of asking, "Why me?" he asks, "What's next?" God opened Clark's eyes to the Gospel, in 1999, when He performed a true miracle, by changing Clark's heart. Clark's eyes were opened to the Word of God, the truth of God, and to what Jesus did for him on the cross.

Clark loved the Lord with all of his heart, and thought he had everything all figured out. But in 2007, he faced some big changes in his life, and Clark is the first to say that he would not have been able to get through that time without the love of the Lord. In July of 2007, Clark was diagnosed with cancer. At the same time his wife left him for another man.

It Is All A Matter Of Focus

Clark had a swollen tonsil, on the left side of his throat, which the doctors determined was cancer. He was given medication and radiation therapy. During that time, he prayed to God, that the growth would be found to be benign, and that God would do a miraculous healing. Although the growth shrunk to about half of its original size, from the medication and radiation therapy, it was still there and it was cancerous.

While all of this was going on, Clark's wife, who had been having an affair, left him for her lover. They were separated while he underwent radiation therapy; then she filed for divorce. Dealing with the cancer alone would have been difficult, but Clark also had to deal with his wife's rejection and the subsequent divorce. It would have been natural for Clark to have felt sorry for himself, focusing on what was happening around him, instead focusing on Jesus. But focusing on Jesus was the only thing that would see him through!

His doctors explained that they could do nothing else for him. They could perform surgery, but that would leave his face terribly disfigured. He did not want that; he was still dealing with rejection from the woman who pledged to love him, through sickness and health.

With all the stress from the radiation and medication therapy, and the heartache of the divorce, Clark lost a lot of weight; but God was right there with him. He had gotten a job two years earlier, with the Post Office, so he had good benefits, with excellent insurance. God had made a way for him to make it through this very difficult time in his life.

Clark made a choice to focus on the wonderful medical benefits, instead of focusing on the problems that were happening in his life. He felt blessed beyond belief that he had insurance and he was able to keep his job. At the same time, he felt blessed to have good friends, who prayed for him.

When his doctors in Billings, Montana, told Clark that there was nothing else they could do for him, they suggested that he should go to a larger metropolitan area, like Houston, or maybe a university hospital. Clark's family is originally from Texas, and he also had a friend, whose father had throat cancer. This man had gone to a doctor at the University of Texas Hospital, in Dallas.

Clark chose to seek out that doctor, and contacted his office, for an appointment. After examining Clark, the doctor felt he could help him without disfiguring his face. This was a tremendous relief to Clark, so he opted for the surgery.

His first surgery took nine hours. After the doctors removed cancerous tissue, it was sent to the lab to determine if they had gotten it all. Each time the report came

It Is All A Matter Of Focus

back indicating some cancer was still left. They cut off a little more and sent it to the lab. The problem was, the doctors could never get what they call 'clear margins', because Clark's throat was so badly burned from the radiation. The doctors were unable to tell what was cancerous, and what was burned from the radiation, so they kept cutting.

Clark had four surgeries, as the medical staff whittled away at the cancer in his throat. Finally, in December of 2008, the only option that remained was to remove all of Clark's tongue, and replace it with a muscle from his abdomen. This was put in place of the tongue, as a flap to protect his airway.

Following the surgery, Clark woke up feeling his tongue was swollen. He had tubes everywhere. As he prayed, he cried out, "Oh Lord, what have they done to me?" He had his eyes closed, and suddenly he was aware of a very bright light in the room. It was so bright that he wondered what was going on. Soon, the light dissipated, and as it did, Clark felt a peace come over him, a peace like he had never felt before. He instantly knew, without a doubt, that everything was going to be alright. He knew that he did not need to worry about anything, because God was in control of the outcome.

It was a long road to recovery. Clark spent eight months at his brother's house, in Texas. The Post Office held his job for him, and his insurance paid for his surgeries. In September of 2009, Clark was able to return to work, but Clark's challenges didn't end then. Recently, he went in for a checkup, and this time, the tests showed a spot on his lungs. With this news, Clark continues to wait for God's direction in his life.

Clark now speaks using an Electro Larynx, which is strapped to his throat. His voice may sound a little different than others', but if you listen closely, Clark's every word can be understood. Far more than the words he chooses, Clark's attitude shines with gratitude. How can he have such gratitude, with all the things he's experienced? Clark's focus is on what Jesus did for him on the cross, and not on the misfortune of divorce, having cancer, or even, his difficulty with talking.

Clark has learned to ask God daily, "What is next?" Life is an ongoing battle with the forces of evil, which do everything possible to take the eyes of the believer away from God and His Will for our lives. Clark knows that everything is in God's hands, for He is sovereign over all. He is in control of Clark's cancer, just like He is in control of the weather.

Clark knows Romans 10:9, which says, "if you confess with your mouth, Jesus is Lord, and believe in your heart that God raised him from the dead, you will be saved". For

Clark, this is much more important than having a tongue, it is more important than anything else, as it should be, for every believer. Everything can be taken from him, but he will always hold on to his faith. He may not be physically healed, until he goes home to heaven with Jesus, but he was spiritually healed, when he gave his life to Jesus.

Clark constantly looks for ways to serve the Lord. At one time, he was involved in a Father and Sons' ministry in Harlowton, Montana. Yet, Clark feels that, without a tongue, he may not be able to serve God effectively. However, God does not look at the outward things of man. He looks at a person's heart, and Clark really has a heart for the things of God. I believe that God has a place of service for Clark, and that Clark will discover it, as he seeks God's will in his life.

Whenever Clark feels sad or depressed, he turns to God, and to His Word, the Bible. This is an application that every believer needs to learn, and apply on a regular basis. One scripture that helps him is 2 Corinthians 4:16-18.

> Therefore we do not lose heart. Though outwardly we are wasting away, yet inwardly we are being renewed day by day. For our light and momentary troubles are achieving for us an eternal glory that far outweighs them

all. So we fix our eyes not on what is seen, but on what is unseen. For what is seen is temporary, but what is unseen is eternal.

There are some who teach that, "if a person has enough faith, God will heal him," and in a way, this is true, but that healing may not come until that person is in heaven with the Lord. We cannot control God, even with our faith; He will heal or not heal, in His own perfect time. Paul, who was one of the greatest men of faith throughout all of time, is a prime example of this.

He talks about it, in 2 Corinthians 12:7-10,

To keep me from becoming conceited because of these surpassingly great revelations, there was given me a thorn in my flesh, a messenger of Satan, to torment me. Three times I pleaded with the Lord to take it away from me. But he said to me, "My grace is sufficient for you, for my power is made perfect in weakness." Therefore I will boast all the more gladly about my weaknesses, so that Christ's power may rest on me. That is why, for Christ's sake, I delight in weaknesses, in insults, in hardships, in persecutions, in difficulties. For when I am weak, then I am strong.

Serving God in our weakness brings glory to God, because we cannot take credit for what He does. When God does not heal us right away, we can easily become depressed, thinking that we did something wrong. In truth, that healing may not come until we are home in heaven, with the Lord.

What God wants is for His people to have faith in Him for Who He is, not just for what He does! If we, as believers, truly focus on God for Who He is, we will never be disappointed, if He chooses not to heal us here on earth. Focusing on God takes our mind off ourselves, and puts our mind on Him, Who is everything good! This, in turn, gives us a good attitude, which can then be clearly seen by others.

Praying for healing that doesn't come may seem unfair. But, God knows what is best for His children, and how He can use the example of His children to reach others for Him.

For God is not fair; He is more than fair!

Things to Ponder

1. Attitude is the one thing that shows, more clearly than anything else, a person's heart. How do you feel about that statement?
2. Instead of asking, "Why me?" Clark asks, "What's next?" Is this a good way to approach a believer's walk with the Lord?
3. While Clark was dealing with cancer his wife left him. How would your attitude be if something like that happened to you? How could you make your attitude better?
4. "Whenever Clark feels sad or depressed, he turns to God, and to His Word, the Bible." How does a person put this into practice?
5. "Serving God in our weakness brings glory to God, because we cannot take credit for what He does." How do you feel about that statement?

14

Lasting Peace

A story is told, about an art teacher who asked his class to paint a picture of peace. Sometime later, he viewed and critiqued the pictures. The first painting he observed depicted the ocean, without a wave, smooth as glass. He congratulated the student on her fine painting. Next, he came upon a painting of a new snowfall, before anything had walked across the landscape, and again, he congratulated the student on his work. So it went that day, as he looked, first at one painting, then the next. Each painting depicted a time of peace, and each student received his congratulations.

Then he came to the last student, whose painting depicted a scene of war. There were bombs bursting everywhere, soldiers shooting guns, soldiers involved in hand-to-hand combat, and chaos all over the battlefield. The teacher looked at the painting, then at the student, asking him if he did not understand the assignment, because he could not see anything to do with peace in this painting.

The student told his teacher that he did indeed understand the assignment. He pointed to a tree, in the middle of the battlefield, and on that tree was a robin, singing a song! He then told his teacher, he believed that, in spite of everything happening around that robin, he was at peace in the midst of conflict, and that was true peace.

The smooth ocean would once again become rough, when the next storm came up. The snowfall would soon be disturbed, when an animal or person came along. True peace comes from a relationship with Jesus, and is a peace within, that lasts!

John Bouchard, of Harlowton, Montana, knows that peace, but it has not always been that way. One day in 1994, John's wife told him she no longer loved him, and wanted a divorce. He felt as though he had been hit; he had not seen it coming, and it had a terrible effect on his life. Not able to understand, he started drinking, which never solves anything, and most of the time makes matters worse.

Lasting Peace

One night, John was out drinking with his brother and sister-in-law, Sharon. They planned to have dinner together later. The bar had some lively music playing, and Sharon asked John to dance with her once before they went for dinner. At the same time, three men were in the middle of a dart game, throwing darts across the dance floor at a dart board. John asked them to stop for the time it would take to have one dance.

These men refused, and kept throwing the darts; one narrowly missed Sharon's head. John was livid, and suggested the man should discuss it with him outside. He later admitted that this was one of the biggest mistakes he had ever made.

John followed the man out the door, but another of them came behind him, striking him as he exited the bar. Two of these three men kicked John in the head, with their boots, while the third one sat on him, striking him in the face. Someone called the Sheriff's office, and the three men were arrested, while John was loaded into an ambulance.

Three days later, John woke up; not in the local hospital, but in a city hospital ninety miles away! The left side of his head was swollen about two inches and he looked a mess. As he woke up, he could feel someone's hand on his. His son,

Brad, was calling for the doctors to hurry in, because his dad was awake.

Brad told his dad he didn't know what was happening, but he heard that John was going to be put in chains — prayer chains! John was thoroughly confused, not even knowing where he was, but he told Brad, if it had something to do with prayer, he should go ask a preacher about those chains. Brad went in search of a preacher, while others entered the hospital room, making John just a little bit nervous, because he still didn't know what was happening.

John's jaws were wired shut in three places and he had a big bandage on his head. He asked the doctor what was going on. The doctor explained that his condition was serious. They had done everything they could. As John thought about how he ended up in the hospital, Brad returned to tell him that the chains people were talking about, were human chains. A group of people are called to pray for someone.

Although John did not know Jesus as Lord, he told Brad that was great, because he knew he was going to need a lot of prayer. The power of prayer is a mighty thing that stirs God into action, and these prayer warriors were praying not just for John's physical needs, but also for his spiritual needs. John's plan was to first get well and then to get even with the men who did this to him. But that plan didn't come to pass. What John really needed, was to know Jesus as Lord and Savior, even though he did not know it at the time. But the prayers went up to God, and a change in his life was on the horizon.

About a week later, the hospital staff removed the tubes and some of the stitches, from John's body, but his mouth was still wired shut, making it difficult for him to speak. He asked one of the nurses about the doctor who had saved his life. He wanted to know where he was, so he could thank him. The nurses explained that the doctor's office was across the street, and he would most likely be there, but John must remain in the hospital, for at least another week.

The minute John was left alone, he removed everything still hooked to him, and proceeded to walk across the street to the doctor's office. There he was, still in his hospital gown, entering the office, when the receptionist asked him what he thought he was doing. She told him that he needed to return to the hospital, and that their staff would wheel him back across the street, in a wheel chair.

John was not about to settle for that, so he marched right into the doctor's office to thank him, even though the doctor was with another patient. The doctor tried putting him off, but John insisted that the doctor give him a minute to talk, telling him, "thank you", for saving his life. The doctor responded that John needed to thank God, because he was never sure if John would make it or not! With that, John was wheeled back to the hospital, thinking he had accomplished what he needed to do.

Before John could be discharged from the hospital, he had to meet with a neurologist for an evaluation of his brain function. The doctor had John watch a screen, which showed different objects, and mark down if he saw a square, a triangle or a circle. After ten of these slides, the neurologist told him he had only gotten three correct. John insisted that he was going home anyway. The doctor told him that he would need to live with someone.

When John told the doctor that he was going to get better, he was told that his condition would either stay the same, or get worse. John was so determined to get better that he even began to pray to the Lord. When he found himself praying the Lord's Prayer, he thought, "Where did that come from?" God often brings to a person's mind things they have heard before, and John had heard this prayer over forty years earlier, in Sunday School.

John returned to Billings once a week, for several more weeks, while he was living with his parents at their ranch. Each time, he saw the neurologist, along with other doctors, for the stitches and wires in his jaw. Soon, the neurologist began to see improvement taking place in John — improvement that he did not expect. He began to test John with multiplication problems. At first, the problems were very simple, but as John answered correctly, the problems became more difficult.

Finally, the neurologist shook his head, telling John he was totally amazed that John was getting so much better, and he could not understand his improvement. John told him that God was doing it, and that God was going to fix him all up! John also informed the doctor that God had performed a miracle in his life, and he was going to tell everyone about it. The neurologist shook his head again, telling John to call it whatever he wanted. For so many, it is hard to acknowledge the work of God in their lives, or in the lives of others.

John spent about three months, with his parents at their ranch and became stronger, both physically and spiritually, with each day. Even though John did not yet know Jesus as his Lord and Savior, God was already doing a mighty work in his life. One day, John decided that it was time for him to start walking outside, even though it was the middle of the winter, in Montana. The first day he made it about 100 yards, when he knew that, if he did not turn back he would not make it back to the house. Each day he walked at least one step further, and when two months had passed, John was up to about three miles, one way!

As time passed, God continued to work on John's heart. He realized that, because of his actions, his sons had spent Christmas in the hospital, wondering if their dad was going to live or die.

He knew that God wanted him to apologize to them, so he called them, asking for their forgiveness. They accepted his apology immediately. John also called his ex-wife, asking her to forgive him, and telling her that he also forgave her. She told John she did not need to be forgiven, because she had done nothing wrong.

Toward the end of February, John's two older sons were playing in a basketball tournament, in Billings, and he felt he needed to go and watch them. He still had bandages, but the need to watch them was great, so he called his friends Russ and Darcy, in Billings, and asked if he could stay with them for a day or two. They welcomed him to come.

Russ was busy, the first night of the tournament, so Darcy drove John to the tournament. The noise of the game gave Darcy a headache, so they left early. As they drove back to the house, Darcy stopped the car, so that she could talk seriously with John. She explained how John could give everything over to Jesus. There, in the midst of tears, John did just that, telling the Lord he just could not handle all the things that had happened in his life.

As he cried, he remembered his upbringing, and how he was taught that real men don't cry. But, as his spirit was opened up to God, the emotions of the situation just came forth. God took all the hurt of the divorce, and everything else that he was dealing with, and replaced it with the joy that comes only from God!

In Romans 5:8, we read, "But God demonstrates his own love for us in this: While we were still sinners, Christ died for us". Knowing that God loved us, even when we were doing all kinds of things that were contrary to His Will, should bring joy to our hearts. In Nehemiah 8:10, we read, "the joy of the LORD is your strength". The true believers find their strength in the joy of the Lord, and the Lord is very joyful, when a person receives Him as Lord and Savior!

When they arrived at Russ and Darcy's home, John could not wait to tell Russ what had just happened in his life! Russ was just coming out of the garage and John ran over to him, started hugging him, and told him that he now knew Jesus was living in him. He told Russ that everything was beautiful, for all that dirty junk was now gone from his mind, and he was going to let Jesus take over his life completely!

By taking Jesus as his Lord and Savior, John was now at peace with God, but would he be able to maintain that peace, with all the things that Satan would bring his way? Satan hates mankind because we are created by God, and made in His image, but he hates the believer even more, because now the believer will spend eternity with God. Now, the war would really start, between John and the forces of evil!

Scripture says, in Ephesians 6:12, "For our struggle is not against flesh and blood, but against the rulers, against the authorities, against the powers of this dark world and against the spiritual forces of evil in the heavenly realms". Because Satan no longer had power over John, he began to attack John through his family. First he started with John's oldest son Shawn, who got involved with the wrong crowd and became addicted to very dangerous drugs. He moved to Seattle, where these drugs were more readily available.

Shawn reached the point that he knew he needed help. John tried to tell him about Jesus, but all Shawn wanted was to go to rehabilitation.

After his time in rehab, Shawn got back in with the wrong crowd again and was soon back into the same life. Nothing had changed. This time, Shawn got even deeper into drugs than before, which of course caused John more heartache. One time, John received a call from the sheriff, telling him to get to the hospital, because Shawn had overdosed. John went to the hospital, and found that Shawn had not only overdosed, but he had also cut his wrists. A father is always a father, and is touched by what his children do, both good and bad. Once again, John had heartache.

John's ex-wife reached the point of saying that she could not take any more of this. She blamed John and herself, and wanted to know what they had done wrong. Parents do that, but Shawn, just like anyone else, had a free will, and made his own choices. Parents can only teach their children the best they know about how to live their lives, but they are not responsible for the choices that their children make.

John did not hear from Shawn for some time; then Shawn called to ask for money. John made the mistake several times, of giving money to Shawn. Doing this just enabled

Shawn to keep on doing what he was doing, without taking responsibility for his actions. John learned about tough love. He still loved Shawn very much, but he could not enable him to continue on this course.

Early one morning, John received a call from the Sheriff's office, telling him that Shawn had been arrested. He was caught stealing drugs from the veterinary clinic, and John thought that maybe, just maybe, that was a good thing. They told John he could come and visit Shawn, which he did. John pleaded with Shawn, to give Jesus a chance to help him. Then he left.

A couple of days later, John received another call from the Sheriff's office. They told him, even though it was not the usual day, or the regular visiting hours, he needed to come up and see his son. A call like this would normally make a person concerned about what could have happened; what had gone wrong now? Instead, on the way to the jail, John felt the Spirit of God reassuring him that something good, something very good, had taken place, and the peace of God came over him!

After he arrived at the jail, John was searched, and then sent down the hall to see Shawn. As he moved toward Shawn, John saw a very happy young man. The Spirit of the Lord

Lasting Peace

shone through Shawn. For the last thirty feet, John prayed like he had never prayed before; John had become a prayer warrior for God. There was a yellow line about three feet from the cell, which no visitor was ever to cross. But as John looked at the deputy, it appeared that he was purposefully looking away, so John crossed that line, and hugged Shawn.

Shawn had just crossed a line too — that line between light and darkness! He told his father that he was higher, right at that time, than he had ever been before, on any drug. He also told John he had been in darkness and now he was in light, and it was so beautiful! Even though Shawn had to pay for the laws of man that he had broken, Jesus had already paid the price for the laws of God that Shawn had broken, and there was rejoicing in heaven!

John became involved as a leader in the youth group of his local church, in Harlowton, Montana. He was a great influencer, in the lives of many young people, and he even had some stay in his home, from time to time.

Jimmy was one of those young people who stayed in John's home, and he became best friends with Shawn. One day, during the winter of 2000-2001, Shawn and Jimmy felt God's call on their lives, to go to the mission field! So they came up with an awesome plan to challenge themselves, by going to work on a fishing boat in Alaska. They had heard that working on an Alaskan fishing boat was one of the roughest types of work there was; it was hard physically, mentally and spiritually. This would be a test they could put themselves through, as they looked to see how God would have them serve Him.

Before Shawn and Jimmy left for Alaska, John spent some time in prayer with them. When they finished praying, John walked them to the car. Shawn turned to John, and told him that if things didn't go the way they planned, he would save John a big fat recliner chair in heaven!

That turned out to be the last time John saw his son, Shawn, here on this earth. On April 2, 2001, John received a call that no father ever wants to receive. The coast guard told him that the boat Shawn and Jimmy were on had gone down, and was lost at sea. The terrible storm that caused the boat to sink also kept the coast guard from conducting a search at the time.

John's youngest son, Brad, was at John's house at that time, so John told him to grab his Bible, and come with him to the church. When Brad asked why, John told him that Shawn's boat had gone down, he was lost at sea, and they needed to go to the church and pray. At the church, they

Lasting Peace

walked around praying, and seeking God's will for Shawn, along with Jimmy, and the others who were lost at sea.

After about an hour of praying, John asked Brad how he was feeling. Brad then told John, that he probably would not believe him, but he was feeling really peaceful. John started crying, and told him that Shawn was not going to come back, for he was resting in the arms of Jesus! God had called Psalms 18:16 to John's mind, which says, "He reached down from on high and took hold of me; he drew me out of deep waters". The deep waters are the earth that we live on, which meant that God had taken Shawn home to be with Him.

God had brought a peace to both Brad and John that could only come from Him. Philippians 4:7 says, "the peace of God, which transcends all understanding, will guard your hearts and your minds in Christ Jesus". With this peace, John and Brad returned to their home, which was soon overrun with fifteen to twenty young people from the youth group. They prayed and cried with John over Shawn. When things began to settle down, one of those young people asked John why he was not still praying. John was the pray warrior of the group, so surely he should still be praying. After all, it was his son they were all praying for.

Then John told them that he was at peace with the situation. He knew where Shawn was and he was not in the depths of the ocean, he was much higher than that. Shawn was in Heaven with Jesus, and Jimmy was right there with him! Both John and Brad were all right with that. In fact, they were more than all right with that, they were praising God!

A funeral service for both Shawn and Jimmy, was held at the High School, in Harlowton. At that service, the Pastor gave a salvation message, and at the end he gave an invitation, asking if anyone wanted to receive Jesus as personal Lord and Savior. That day, over one hundred people gave their hearts to the Lord!

Even before Shawn went to Alaska, several family members gave their hearts to the Lord, for they could see the change Jesus had made, in both John and Shawn's lives, and they wanted to have that too.

John was once a person who did not really know any kind of peace. But now, he was able to experience peace in the midst of conflict. The only reason that John was able to come to the point of knowing that lasting peace, is because God is not fair, He is more than fair!

Things to Ponder

1. Can a person ever find peace in this world?
2. As time passed John realized that he needed to apologize to his sons. There are times when each believer needs to apologize to people he/she has hurt in the past, but this is not easy. How can the believer make this happen? Is there anyone you need to apologize to?
3. What is the only thing a person can do when a loved one is not living like he or she should be?
4. "Satan hates mankind because we are created by God, and made in His image, but he hates the believer even more." Does this statement bring peace or fear to your mind?
5. How could John be at peace with the knowledge that he would never see Shawn again in this world?

15

Jesus Loves Even Me

*W*hen Jesus was asked, what is the greatest commandment? He replied, "Love the Lord your God with all your heart and with all your soul and with all your mind and with all your strength.' The second is this: `Love your neighbor as yourself.' There is no commandment greater than these". (Mark 12:30-31) I taught this passage one Sunday morning in a church I once pastored. One of the women in the congregation told me that she did not love herself, in fact she did not even like herself, so how could she love her neighbor as herself?

Many people, in the church today, are in the same situation. For one reason or another, they have a very low sense of self-esteem, and therefore, have trouble loving others. This low self-esteem could be a result of many different things, but whatever the cause, these people have a distorted opinion of themselves.

I once knew a man with low self-esteem, because he never felt loved by his parents. He just didn't measure up in their eyes. It's natural for parents to love their children; when this does not happen, children will most certainly have low self-esteem.

Low self-esteem can be the result of being teased about physical features — if they are too heavy or too thin, have a large nose, crooked teeth, or any number of other things. If they are made fun of for such features, or even for how they act; and it can affect how they feel about themselves. I remember a girl in school, who was ridiculed and taunted, because of the size of her nose; it had a tremendously negative effect on her self-esteem.

How a person does in the classroom can also have a major effect on that person's self-esteem. I was the youngest of three boys and I was constantly asked by my teachers, why I didn't do as good of a job with my studies as my brothers had. At times, I did not think very highly of myself, and therefore, did not care if I did a good job in school, or not. Then I had a teacher who was an encourager and he changed my life. He taught me that I was someone special and I was worth a great deal. How thankful I am for that teacher! But not everyone has someone like him.

Liz Awe is a friend of mine, who had suffered for a very long time with low self-esteem. She grew up as a Pastor's daughter, and always knew in her mind that God loved her. The problem was that even though she knew in her head that God loved her, she did not believe it in her heart. As a teenager, she suffered from extremely low self-esteem, and it carried over into her adulthood.

About the time her family moved to Rapid City, South Dakota, the Lord spoke to her heart saying, "Love your neighbor as yourself". (Mark 12:31) She felt that she really could not love anyone else like that, because she disliked herself so very much. Scripture says, in Philippians 1:6 "He who began a good work in you will carry it on to completion until the day of Christ Jesus". Therefore, God was not about to leave her in this state of mind.

So how do people go from a state of loathing themselves to one of self-worth? What is required is to see oneself through God's eyes and that means looking into His Word. Early in the Bible, we see that all of mankind is created in

His image. God speaking, in Genesis 1:26 says, "Let us make man in our image, in our likeness, and let them rule over the fish of the sea and the birds of the air, over the livestock, over all the earth, and over all the creatures that move along the ground". His sole purpose of doing this was to have fellowship with you.

Then there is the fact that, even though man chose to sin and fall away from God, He provides a way for that fellowship to be renewed. Scripture tells us that "God demonstrates his own love for us in this: While we were still sinners, Christ died for us". (Romans 5:8) We also see, in John 3:16, "God so loved the world that he gave his one and only Son, that whoever believes in him shall not perish but have eternal life". In 1 John 4:10, we read, "this is love: not that we loved God, but that he loved us and sent his Son as an atoning sacrifice for our sins".

If Liz had been the only one that needed salvation, Jesus would have died for her, just as if you were the only one who needed salvation, Jesus would have died for you. By learning that God loved her that much, Liz was able to become a person of worth, both in the eyes of the Lord, and in her own eyes, which made a major change in how Liz interacted with people. God had given her the ability to love people, and He then used this to draw them closer to Him, by using her as His instrument of love.

As a result of the low self-esteem, Liz also suffered from extreme shyness, and God brought her out of that. When her children were little, she worked part-time as a church secretary, and God opened up the door for her to sell candles in people's homes. This meant that she was going to have to talk to people that she didn't know; and it scared her to death.

God had opened the door for her to sell these candles, and she had a great sense that she needed to do it, even though it would be very difficult for her. God does this very often in the life of the believer, so that He can grow us into what He wants us to be, and He uses that experience to bring glory to Himself. Liz sold candles to help pay the bills, but God used it to give her the ability to talk to people, without the pain of dealing with her shyness. He also developed in her, a whole set of people skills she would need in following His plan for her life.

After graduating from high school, Liz attended Bible College for two years, because it seemed to her that was what she was supposed to do at that point in her life. She graduated with an associate degree, but she did not come away with anything that she wanted to pursue as her life's work. She went back home, met the man she would spend her life with, got married, and became an active lay person in her church.

As lay people in their local church, Liz and her husband endeavored to support their Pastor, no matter who he or she was. One thing Pastors need, is to feel that their church is supportive of their leadership. Ministry is being used by God to touch people's hearts for Him and without a supportive church, it becomes a job instead of a joy.

Liz worked as Church Secretary over the years for several different Pastors. Each told her that she really had a Pastor's heart.

A Pastor is called to shepherd a Church, therefore a Pastor needs to have the heart of a shepherd. Having the heart of a Pastor involves caring more about others than anything else, taking time to get to know them, and loving them with the love of God, even when it seems that they are unlovable. It means doing what is best for the church, even if it is not the most popular thing to do. It also means speaking God's truth in love, without ever compromising His truth.

At one point in her life, Liz's family was part of the launch team, as her church worked to plant a daughter church. This opened up new horizons for her, but also a new responsibility, which was very trying for her. Her Pastor had asked her to be in charge of the Worship Team, as Worship Pastor and that brought a considerable amount of conflict into her life.

On this worship team, were a few individuals with strong personalities, who opposed Liz often, making her job as Worship Leader very difficult. God teaches, in Scripture, believers are to "obey your leaders and submit to their authority" (Hebrews 13:17), and yet so many Christians fail to do this. One of the biggest reasons for this is, people forget that what they, as individuals, want is not important. It's what God wants to accomplish through them, that is the most important thing in a believer's life. This involves submitting to God, by submitting to the person or people, that He has placed over them.

Dealing with difficult situations is never easy, but through that time of conflict, Liz began to see God's plan for her life. She was beginning to have a great sense that she was to continue in that position. As a result of that, she knew the only thing she could do was to keep committing it to God, and when those difficult situations arose, to commit it to God, commit it to God, and then commit it to God!

As Liz learned to commit things to God, He began to work in other areas of her life. At one point, she was struggling with something that caused her to be jealous, and she felt the Lord telling to her that she needed to release it. Ever since man first sinned, people have thought that they must be in control of their lives, but when a person submits to God, then He is given Lordship of that life and jealousy has no part in it.

Liz, just like most of us, felt a need to be in control of her life, and she believed that by doing so, she would be able to attain some self-worth. As she continued to search for that feeling of significance, the Holy Spirit came over her, like she had never felt it before. She finally surrendered to God, allowing Him to be totally in control of her life, and for the first time she felt significant in His eyes. The Creator of the world loved her, as she had never been loved before!

Sometime after Liz had been asked to be Worship Pastor, Pastor Scott approached her about pursuing ordination. It was not until that point that she began to put everything together.

Bible College, serving as a Church Secretary, selling candles, and being Worship Pastor were all preparation for

God's calling on her life to be an ordained Pastor of the Wesleyan Church.

Liz was struck with the realization that God indeed did have an overall plan for her life and all those things were His training for her calling of a lifetime. All she could do was sit back and say, "WOW," for God had been at work and was continuing to work in her life, making her something special, in His awesomeness and in His kingdom.

Liz faced another major challenge in her life, during the winter of 2009-2010. She had a bad sinus infection, which she tried to cure with over-the-counter medication. On Wednesday, March 3rd, she had a really bad earache. She felt very dizzy and she couldn't think clearly. She went to the doctor, who gave her a prescription which she immediately had filled. Then she went home, collapsed into bed and went to sleep.

Sleep is always good, when a person does not feel well, but on Thursday morning, when Liz's husband attempted to wake her for work, she was unresponsive. As the day went on, Liz's condition continued to get worse and worse. Around 5:00 that evening, her husband again tried to wake her and it was at that point, he called 911, for an ambulance, to take her to the hospital. After some testing, it was found that the sinus infection had gotten so bad that it had gone into her brain and Liz was diagnosed with meningitis!

Meningitis is an inflammation of the membranes that cover the brain and spinal cord, which are known as the meninges. It is usually caused by an infection and it can be life-threatening, because the inflammation is close to the brain and spinal cord. It is classified as a medical emergency and needs to be treated immediately.

Liz was heavily sedated from the beginning, because she kept trying to pull the tubes out that the hospital staff had attached to her. Other than that, she made no response of any sort to what was happening to her. At one point, Liz's husband was told that IF she ever woke up, she would probably have some kind of disability. She might not be able to walk and maybe not even able to think or reason.

There was even the possibility that she could die and this knowledge was quite difficult for her family to handle. Her daughter feels everything very deeply, so she was really worried about her mother. Although this young girl knew that God had the situation in His hands, she was devastated, as she thought of the possibility of losing her mother. It is so hard not to know, if someone you love is going to live or die.

Word had gone out to the body of believers and they went to their knees in prayer. That Sunday, her Church devoted most of the service to praying for her. There were people all over, who were lifting her name before the Lord and He was about to move in a mighty way!

On Monday morning, the District Board was to meet. Liz took care of the books for the District, and she had prepared some of the reports early, which was going to make it easier for that meeting, as Liz would not be there. The board felt a strong need to pray for Liz, instead of just starting their meeting, so they prayed with all their hearts for God to do a miracle. As these men and women of God prayed, God moved in a mighty way, touching Liz's body and healing her!

They were praying, at 9:00 AM, when Liz woke up. Her husband, Dean, began talking to her about how things would have to be a little different and some of the changes they would need to make. But, Liz was having none of that! At the same time, Liz had a tremendous sense, that God wasn't going to do things half-way; but He was indeed, going to do a complete miracle healing in her life!

God is not fair; He is more than fair! Liz's recovery was a quick thing! On Monday, she woke up and by Friday, she was checked out of the hospital and went home! In just two short weeks, Liz returned to work! Although she had a little trouble at first, she is a walking miracle!

What God did for Liz, has been a great encouragement for a lot of people, because they now know someone for whom God had done a miracle, as a direct result of their faithful prayer to Him. Also, one of her doctors told her that she was sure an interesting read. When she thanked him, he replied, "You don't want to be an interesting read, medically!" He then reassured her that the tests he did showed she was, indeed, healed, which was totally amazing! Liz serves a God who gave her much more than she deserved, because He is not fair, He is more than fair!

Things to Ponder

1. Do you love yourself? Do you know that Jesus loves you? How are you doing about loving your neighbor?
2. How should a person treat others so they will feel that they are loved? Is there ever a time when the believer is justified for not loving a sinner?
3. At one time or another everyone thinks they need to be in control of their lives, but who should really be in control? Have you given the reins of your life over to God?
4. Liz was struck with the realization that God indeed did have an overall plan for her life. Have you come to the realization that God has a plan for your life too? Have you discovered what that plan is?
5. The prayers went up to heaven for Liz and she was healed. Do you believe in the power of prayer? Have you experienced the power of prayer in your life?

16

Bootstrap Mentality

*I*n the western part of the United States, a lot of people believe in bootstrapping! Bootstrapping, or bootstrap mentality, means that I can do anything by myself. These people believe that "if a man can't pull himself up by his own bootstraps, then he is not much of a man." Bootstrap thinking (I can do anything just because I want to) leads to the belief that I determine my own destiny.

This perspective, that a real man is a self-made man, goes against what the Scripture says, "I can do everything through Him who gives me strength". (Philippians 4:13) Did you get that last part? I can do anything; but it's not on my own strength – it is through Jesus. It is a belief, either in Jesus, or not in Jesus, that determines my destiny.

When Steve Helms was a teenager growing up in Wyoming, his family went camping for their summer vacation. One year, they were close to Dubois, Wyoming, where Steve loved to fish. He knew a spot where there was sure to be some pretty good fishing. Like most teenagers in the west, Steve thought that he was bullet proof! He was sure he could do anything and not get hurt.

To get to this fishing hole, he had to cross the Wiggins fork of the Wind River and Steve was about to learn that he wasn't 'bullet proof'. Even though the water was fairly low, it had just melted off the snow fields, therefore it was very cold. Steve decided to cross at the top of a big pool, which was between 60 and 70 yards long, and around twelve feet deep. He was in the middle of the river, when his feet were swept out from under him and he went down.

He was carrying a couple of fishing rods in his left hand, and a tackle box in his right hand, as he went under. The cold water rushed in, taking his breath away, as he could not touch bottom or get to the top. He bobbed along, for the full length of the pool, wondering to himself, if he was going to live or die. When he reached the end of the pool, he managed to get to the other side of the river and climb out. Right then and there, he gained a new perspective about being bullet proof!

Although Steve did not drink alcohol or take other drugs in his years of high school, he still had the attitude that he could do just about anything that he wanted to do. He was heavily involved in sports and liked playing basketball in particular. One day, his basketball coach, who saw great potential in Steve, asked him if he was interested in going to the Air Force Academy. Steve responded that he did not need the discipline. This was a decision that would come back to bite him, for discipline was exactly what he really needed in his life!

When he was in high school, Steve was able to get good grades with little or no studying. Then he went off to college, at South Dakota School of Mines, in Rapid City, South Dakota. There he expected to be able to do the same. He thought college was just an extension of high school. In college, the teachers expect their students to be able to study, to produce, to understand what is being taught and thereby build upon one's academic experiences. This was another lesson that Steve had to learn the hard way.

His plan, when he first started attending the School of Mines, was to play basketball. He was very good at it, and surely the coach would give him a scholarship, equivalent to his skills! The trouble was, the coach was not willing to give Steve that scholarship, so he decided not to play at all. Also, he did not spend much time 'doing that school thing', because the grades would just come. But they didn't! He ended with a few Cs, a few Ds and he even failed one class. He then realized that maybe, just maybe, he should spend a little more time studying the books, and a lot less time playing around. Finally, he decided that he should leave the School of Mines, and transfer back to the University of Wyoming, at Laramie.

Steve's girlfriend was also going to school at the University of Wyoming, so he thought that things were going to finally work out for him. He made it through his first year at the University of Wyoming, but the Dean of the engineering program called him into the office. The Dean informed him that he needed to straighten up and work, or he was going to be kicked out of the engineering program. To make life even more challenging, he didn't have a summer job and his girlfriend broke up with him.

Bootstrap Mentality

It was around the first of June, when Steve began to wonder if his life would ever turn around. His family was living at Lusk, Wyoming, so he decided to go north of town, where the Oregon Trail crosses Wyoming, and think about his situation. He contemplated what he should be doing with his life, but he came to the conclusion that he had no idea.

Then Steve did something he would remember the rest of his life: He cried out to God saying, "God, if You're out there, I need You! I need You to make my life meaningful! I need You to take control of my life and help me get things straightened out, because I've made a mess of it!"

This was the turning point of his life, as he reached out to the only One who could ever straighten out his life. Steve felt like a burden had been lifted off his shoulders, an experience that no man or woman can understand, unless he or she has experienced it personally. It's like when a person sees new grass in the spring, that person has hope summer is not far away. Steve began reading his Bible and discovering new insights about the Creator of the universe!

Soon after that, Steve met a man named Jack, who worked in the oil field at Lance Creek, Wyoming. Jack was not sure if he was going to hire any help that summer, but Steve began pestering him, and finally Jack offered Steve a job, which Steve readily accepted. Jack and his wife, Carol, are phenomenal Christians, and grounded in the Word, and Steve started attending services with them, at the Christian Missionary Alliance Church of Lance Creek. Steve grew in the Lord, as he united himself with these believers, and whenever he was home from college, he attended church at Lance Creek.

At the end of that first summer, as Steve prepared to return to school, Jack told him he was welcome to come back and work for him the next summer. It had been a very rewarding experience for him; it felt just like home away from home. Steve worked for Jack every summer, of the four years he was in college.

School at the University of Wyoming was no walk in the park. Steve put his nose to the grindstone and started to get his act together. In the oil field, he enjoyed the variety of his work, which he found very rewarding. Getting that engineering degree, however, continued to be a very challenging path. Gas Dynamics Class, in particular, was quite difficult for him, because he just didn't quite understand what was being taught.

One day, Steve was looking up at the sky, and he told God, if He would help him through that class, so he could graduate, he would do anything that God asked him to do, even be a preacher! God looked at Steve's heart, which was a heart for God, and helped him through that class, with a C, so he could graduate. God looks at the heart of man, not what he says he will do or not do; and then He works His perfect plan in that person's life. And God had plans for Steve's life! That is not to say that Steve would be like a puppet in God's hands, for God always allows each person to choose to follow, or not to follow Him.

During his time at the University of Wyoming, Steve met the woman he would spend the rest of his life with. Darla is a very strong Christian woman, from Powell Wyoming, so Steve wasted no time proposing to her! She accepted, and they were married in August of 1984. After their marriage, Steve had one more year of college, but Darla had already graduated and gotten a job as an electrical engineer. Her job kept her traveling around the country, which made for a difficult time for these newlyweds, but they were able to be together on most weekends.

Darla's job took her to Cody, Wyoming, in January of 1985, and when Steve graduated in May, he moved there, as well. About that time, the whole country suffered with an oil crunch, making it difficult for Steve to find an engineering job in Cody. The only job he could find was working for the Forest Service that year, which he found to be very interesting work.

The trouble was that Steve and Darla did not have the same days off, so they had to make the best of each and every minute they had together. During the first two years of marriage, Steve and Darla spent a total of about three months together, but they were both really committed to making their marriage work. If these two people had relied just on themselves, their marriage most likely would have fallen apart, but they built their marriage with Jesus at its center, which caused it to succeed!

God began to work in Steve's heart, asking him to make small changes in his life. God always allows a person to make his/her own choices, but He does give guidance to the believer. Steve was a very avid hunter, hunting everything that he could. It didn't matter if it was deer, elk, antelope, birds or even rabbits; Steve would not miss a chance to hunt. He hunted every day of the week, if he could. The Holy Spirit began to work on his attitude, causing him to decide to give the Lord His due on Sunday, so Steve quit hunting on Sunday.

That is how God works in the life of a believer; He gently guides the believer into making changes in his or her life, growing that believer into becoming more and more like Jesus. Steve would see many more changes take place in his life, as he grew in Christ. In 1991, Darla had an opportunity for a job in Billings, Montana, which she was very excited about. Steve had been playing Mr. Mom to their daughter, as he was working only part time for an engineering firm in Cody. They sold their home in Cody and moved to Billings, which was a very positive move for them.

Soon after they arrived in Billings, they began attending the Church of God, but in time that church closed, so they started looking for a new church. They found a little Wesleyan Church in Billings Heights, and attended one Sunday morning. They immediately felt at home, which is not typical for a first time visitor at any church. Then just a few days later, the Pastor visited them in their home, which cemented their relationship with this church. This was almost twenty years ago and they are still going strong.

Steve's pastor was instrumental in helping him to solidify his relationship with the Lord. He urged Steve to go to a Promise Keepers meeting in Seattle, Washington, at the Kingdome. It changed his life! As John Maxwell, who is a powerful man of God, spoke, the Lord began dealing with Steve, about several issues. When John Maxwell gave an altar call, Steve went forward, as the Holy Spirit spoke to his heart. That time in his life really cemented his relationship with the Lord!

Shortly after that, Steve's church (East Gate Wesleyan Church of Billings, Montana,) started a children's ministry they called Kingdom Kids Club. Children from around that part of the town attended, where they learned how to pray, memorized scripture, and ended with a Bible story. Steve was asked to tell the Bible story, which was an interesting challenge for him. He began by using a flannel graph, but he found that it was very difficult to hold the children's attention. After one or two stories, the children seemed to get bored and restless, so Steve knew he needed to make some changes, if this was going to affect those children's lives.

He knew he had to do something to hold their interest, but what could he do? The Holy Spirit spoke to his heart and Steve began to use a regular drawing tablet, drawing out the story as he told it. It worked, and he was able to hold the attention of those children all the way through the Bible story!

Steve has been sharing Bible stories for the last seventeen years, occasionally using the flannel graph, for a little variety and sometimes, just telling the story. He has been able to hold the attention of the children and even their parents, most of the time.

Working with children or adults can become frustrating at times, and Satan will cause even the strongest Christians to doubt that they are being effective for God. We wonder if we are making any difference in the lives of those God has called us to serve. What is really important is not what a person does, but what God does through that person!

At times, God reveals to a believer how He has used them to change someone's life. This was exactly what transpired in Steve's life! God began to reveal to him the transformation that had taken place in a few of the children, when he had told them Bible stories.

One day, the director of Kingdom Kids Club shared one such story with Steve: The family of a boy who had sat through Steve's storytelling, had moved to Plentywood, Montana. The director had run into that boy's mother, in Billings. His mother told the director she didn't know what they had done to her son, but he was a changed kid! He was now pleasant around the house, he now wanted to do things to help at home, and he even made his own bed. This mother attributed all of the change to those who worked with her son, at Kingdom Kids Club!

A few years later, Steve 'just happened' to run into a young lady who had been in Kingdom Kids Club, from kindergarten through sixth grade. I say, 'just happened', because there are no coincidences with God; with God everything happens for a reason. God had another story that Steve needed to hear, so he would know that God was blessing the work of Kingdom Kids Club.

That young lady was attending another church in Billings, and was then in a young adults class. The teacher was trying to tell a Bible story to that class and she was really having a difficult time, because she really had no idea what she was talking about. Then that young lady got up, and told the entire story from memory, including explaining the meaning to the rest of the class. She knew this story because she had heard Steve tell it at Kingdom Kids Club. Even though Steve was a little shocked when she told him that, he was also reassured that God was making a difference in those children's lives, and He was using Steve to do it!

Very seldom do we know how God has used us to orchestrate change in the people around us. God says in the Bible, "so is my word that goes out from my mouth: It will not return to me empty, but will accomplish what I desire and achieve the purpose for which I sent it". (Isaiah 55:11) God continually works through the lives of believers, touching hearts and changing lives. We, as believers, must trust Him to accomplish what He wants through us.

Things have changed over the years, at East Gate Wesleyan Church, but the ministry to children is still going strong, although they have made a few changes in it. The program has more of a club atmosphere, and the name has been changed to 'FROG Club', which stands for 'Fully Rely On God'! Steve is still spending his time teaching children Bible stories and touching lives for Jesus.

Steve has seen this children's ministry impact the lives of his own children. Both his daughter and his son are well grounded in the Word. They have become Christians, and have made commitments to the Lord, all because of the Frog Club and a few other events in their lives.

Steve often remembers that time, outside of the engineering building at the University of Wyoming, when he told God he would do anything for Him, even be a Preacher!

Steve IS a preacher in a way. He teaches the Word of God to children, and even gets a chance to touch the life of an adult every so often! Several of the children who come to Frog Club, do not go to any church on a regular basis. On occasion, the parents of those children come to see what goes on at Frog Club. A lot of those parents end up sitting through Steve's teaching of a Bible story, and hearing the Word of God preached through that story.

Steve enjoys working with children so much! He is also involved with the 4H club, where he helps children in countless ways. He teaches them about building displays for the fair and doing woodworking projects. Steve's passion is still archery, so he also teaches that, to his 4H students. Young people even learn to build their own archery equipment from Steve, as he teaches them the right way to make and use that equipment.

Over the years, several different people have been mentors to Steve. They have had a tremendous effect on his life. Now Steve uses his God-given talents, to help others learn to be just what God wants them to be!

One of the scriptures Steve uses, to encourage people, is found in Proverbs 3:5-6, which says, "Trust in the LORD with all your heart and lean not on your own understanding; in all your ways acknowledge him, and he will make your paths straight". That doesn't mean that a person is not going to have a few difficult times in life, and some obstacles to overcome. The key thing is to <u>keep trusting in God</u>, because without trust, there is not a cemented relationship with Him!

This would not seem fair, to people who believe in bootstrap mentality, because they want to trust only in themselves. Scripture says, in Matthew 6:33, "But seek first his kingdom and his righteousness, and all these things will be given to you as well". What we cannot do on our own, we can do, by trusting in the Lord! Once again, I must say that God is not fair, He is more than fair!

Things to Ponder

1. Is it possible to be a true follower of Jesus and believe in bootstrapping?
2. Where the Oregon Trail crosses Wyoming, Steve cried out to the Lord, turning his life over to the only one who could straighten it out. Where were you and how did you become a believer in Jesus or have you?
3. Steve met a couple who were phenomenal Christians and they along with others discipled him. Who discipled you in your walk with the Lord? Who are you in turn discipling?
4. God gifts each and every believer; Steve is using his gifts to teach young people. How are you using your gifts? Whose heart is Jesus using you to touch?
5. "At times, God reveals to a believer how He has used them to change someone's life." Has God revealed to you how He has used you and if so how so?

17

One In A Million

*Y*ears ago, when I was in college, I took a math course in Probability. This course dealt with the chances of random events happening. For instance, if you have 4 red marbles and 6 blue marbles in a jar, the probability of randomly pulling out a red marble is 4 in 10. Duane Neprud of Billings, Montana, would have really enjoyed that course because he is a numbers man. Probability, statistics and all things related to math, really speak to him. When the Holy Spirit speaks to the heart of a person, He always uses those things that impress that person. God used probability to get Duane's attention.

Duane was not raised in church, but his parents left it up to him to make his own choice on whether to go or not. They didn't push church, but every now and then they might attend on Easter or Christmas. Their next door neighbor in Minneapolis, Minnesota, taught him Sunday School lessons in her home, out of the kindness of her heart. But even that did not move him toward a relationship with the Lord.

In December of 1992, God spoke to Duane's heart in a different way. He was working for Bearing Supply Company, at 1123 2nd Avenue North, Billings, Montana. Just before 5:00 PM, on December 18^{th,} Duane decided to make a run to the Post Office, in the company pickup. This was the first time, in about six months, he had made that run, and as he left, a disaster was about to take place.

As Duane drove back to work, from the Post Office, he saw a big column of smoke in the form of a mushroom cloud, coming up into the clear blue sky. It was a cold, sunny winter day, and that column of smoke looked bazaar. The closer he got to his work location, the more it appeared to be right where he worked! Add to that, there were ambulances, police cars and sheriff's cars passing him, traveling in the same direction, as he drove down 2nd Avenue.

Duane noticed that the emergency personnel were already closing off the area around the city block where he worked. Immediately, he wondered what was going on. What happened? A twin-engine jet, carrying six employees of the Western Area Power Administration, along with two pilots, had crashed into the ground right on the street, within 75 yards of the office where Duane would have normally been working!

The plane hit the pavement, slid into the school district's warehouse, and severed a two inch gas line, which caused a fire in that warehouse. On a normal Friday afternoon, that warehouse would have had a lot of people in it, but most of them had gotten off early. Only three remained, and they all escaped without injury. The building, which was packed with paper, ink and chemicals, burned to the ground. However, all eight passengers on the plane, perished in the crash.

A few days later, Duane began to think of the probability of what had taken place that fateful Friday, in December 1992. Let's say for each random event there is one chance out of 100 of it happening, then for each succeeding event the chances are multiplied together, making it one chance in 10,000. What are the chances of a plane crashing? What are the chances that it crashes in broad daylight, in the street, right next to the building where Duane works? What are the chances that, for the first time in six months, Duane is not at work at that time? What are the chances that the warehouse has only three employees working at that time of day? A very conservative answer for all those events taking place at the same time, would be <u>one in a million</u>!

With this information in hand, Duane was awe struck, as he thought, "Why wasn't I there?" Eight people died that day, right in front of where Duane worked while he was out driving around the streets of Billings. He could have arrived back at work, at that exact time, but he didn't.

About that time, another event took place in Duane's life which also made him wonder. At that point, Duane and his wife, Larae, had been married for about five years. They had one child, an adopted son. They had been told by doctors that they would be unable to have their own children, but nine months and five days after the plane crash, Larae gave birth to a healthy baby boy. They named him Steven.

This really got Duane's attention, as he thought about the fact, that first he was not at work at the time the plane crashed, and now they had a new member in their family. What are the chances of those two events happening so close together? Duane knew, without a doubt, that he just was not that lucky. Duane found himself holding that precious gift from God and thinking to himself, "WOW!"

Duane knew in his heart that it was time to step up to the plate, and be responsible for this beautiful bundle of joy, but he didn't know if he could. He found himself subconsciously asking God for help, even though he really did not know God. He knew about God, but did not have a personal relationship with Him.

When Steven was born, Duane and Larae's adopted son, Truman, was 14. A short time later, Truman's best friend, Andy, invited him to attend the youth group at East Gate Wesleyan Church. Soon the entire Neprud family was attending church services. At that time, Duane was struggling with how he was going to raise two boys, so far apart in age. One would be in diapers, while the other one would soon be taking drivers' education!

As time passed, Larae began to notice the effect the church had on Duane. She even told him that she liked him better, after he came home from church, than the rest of the time. Something was happening to him that she really liked. On Easter Sunday, 1995, East Gate Wesleyan Church showed the Jesus Film. Duane watched that film with a few other people, and prayed to receive Jesus, at the end of the movie.

He didn't say a word to anyone, but just wanted to reflect on what he had done, so he got in his car and drove away. He had driven about two blocks, two very long blocks, when he came to a stop sign. There, he told the Lord he had really messed up his life, to this point; but now he was ready to have Jesus come into his life and take control!

For quite some time, God had been manifesting Himself in Duane's life, in physical, tangible ways. Duane had experienced things that just should not have happened, but they did. These things were as clear to Duane as the nose on his face, or the clothes he was wearing! One might have been a coincidence, but not so many. God had been preparing Duane for a meeting that took place at that stop sign, just two blocks from his church! It was as if God was saying to Duane, "HEY DUDE, I WANT YOU!"

Duane kept attending church, and people began to notice him and his family. Soon he was asked to co-teach an adult Sunday School Class. As he thought about it, he realized that he was a young man, in his early 30s, and there would be people in the class who had read the Bible from cover to cover. He thought to himself that he was a baby Christian, who hadn't even read the entire New Testament and he was being asked to teach these 'pillars of the faith'. How could he do it? He prayed, "Oh Lord, what have I gotten myself into?" The only thing he could do was to tell the church he would pray about it. He mulled it over in his mind, thinking that he didn't know how to teach. He was very reluctant to accept the position.

A few days later, Duane was delivering parts in his job at Bearing Supply. He asked the Lord to show him what he should do. He wanted the Lord to make it so clear to him that he would not have a doubt, as to whether he was to teach or not. He had made his deliveries in Laurel, and came back to Billings, to his first stop there.

He pulled up to the loading dock, and started to get out of the truck to unload, when suddenly an interesting thing happened. It was a good thing he was not driving at the time, because he might have been in an accident! The presence of the Holy Spirit filled the cab of the truck, to such an extent that He got Duane's total attention! This was just a half an hour after he had asked the Lord for a sign on what to do, about the teaching invitation. There were no words spoken, just the manifestation of the Presence of God, which literally increased the air pressure inside the cab of the truck. He knew, right then and there, that he was to teach, and he has been teaching ever since!

Many people feel unqualified to teach the Word of God. If they don't have formal training, they leave it up to others. But the truth is, we learn from what we teach. No one likes to be embarrassed, by a lack of knowledge, so a teacher works hard to learn the material before presenting it to others. Also, a teacher should never be afraid to admit that he or she doesn't know everything!

When the Israelites entered the Promised Land, they had to show a step of faith to cross the Jordan River. Joshua 3:15-17 says,

> Now the Jordan is at flood stage all during harvest. Yet as soon as the priests who carried the ark reached the Jordan and their feet touched the water's edge, the water from upstream stopped flowing. It piled up in a heap a great distance away, at a town called Adam in the vicinity of Zarethan, while the water flowing down to the Sea of the Arabah (the Salt Sea) was completely cut off. So the people crossed over opposite Jericho. The priests who carried the ark of the covenant of the LORD stood firm on dry ground in the middle of the Jordan, while all

Israel passed by until the whole nation had completed the crossing on dry ground.

Not until the priest's feet hit the water's edge, did the Jordan stop flowing. In the same way, for whatever God has called you to do, He will provide the necessary tools to get that job done, but not until you are ready to take that step of faith. God equips those He has called!

God moved in Duane's life, equipping him for his journey as a true follower. He used several methods and events to teach Duane, one of which was the big spiritual movement for men, called Promise Keepers. One weekend, a group of men from East Gate Wesleyan Church, piled into some vans and drove to Seattle for a conference. Duane drove late into the night, and one of the men offered to sit up front and help keep him awake, as he drove across the state of Washington. However, as Duane drove, that man in the passenger seat snored like a bear, and Duane had no problem keeping awake! For nearly 100 miles, Duane laughed his head off, as the other man snored away, making that drive seem just a little bit shorter.

Promise Keepers is a great spiritual movement, which brings revival to the hearts of many men. It touches the emotions of a lot of men, setting them on fire for the Lord. As John Maxwell preached the Word of God, Duane felt that his own heart was replaced with the heart of God. He knew that something important was happening; it was amazing. Promise Keepers is an extremely large part of spiritual growth for many men, and Duane is one of them!

One year, Duane took his father along to Promise Keepers, and he was blessed to witness him, praying to receive Jesus, as his Lord and Savior! Another time, Duane was among the volunteers whose job was to talk with the men who came forward, during the altar call. He witnessed men who were so touched by the Holy Spirit; their hearts softened so much that tears just streamed down their faces, right before his eyes. Just to be part of that, to be used by God in such a special way, touched his heart like nothing else could!

It was not because of some special ability that he had, but because God called him to be there and he was willing to do whatever the Holy Spirit prompted him to do. God continually uses ordinary people to do His Will, but He requires a willingness to follow Him, wherever He leads. The choice to follow, or not to follow, is yours, but the outcome is His. God will accomplish His will, and if the believer is not willing to follow His lead, then He will get someone else.

Several other people have come to Jesus, because of God's work in Duane's life. People watch Christians to see if, what they say they believe, shows in how they live their lives. The way a believer lives and treats others, has a tremendous effect on the lives of others. How much the Christian loves Jesus, is shown in how much that Christian loves the least lovable, of the people he or she knows!

During the summer of 2011, Duane had an accident, riding on an ATV, while on vacation, visiting family. He wrecked the ATV and hurt his shoulder by tearing his rotator cuff. This accident put him out of work for a few months. He no longer worked for Bearing Supply, but worked in a job that required him to lift 40 pounds continuously, all day long, for ten hour shifts. The doctors told him he would be better in three months, but for that kind of work, rehabilitation could take up to a year!

The union contract he worked under had sick pay, but that lasted only so long. Short-term disability paid just a fraction of what his normal pay was, and his wife worked only a part-time job, so their finances were very tight. Duane knew that scripture says, in Philippians 4:19, "God will meet all your needs according to his glorious riches in Christ Jesus". Still he wondered how they would make it, on only a fourth of what they normally had to live on? By all calculations, they would run out of money and have to borrow from friends and family, just to get by until he returned to work.

There was nothing that Duane or his wife could do about the situation, but trust in God. Men, more than women, have a hard time sometimes, trusting God to provide, because God has put in them the desire to provide for their families. It is one of the things that makes a man, a man!

When Duane was finally brought low enough, where he could not do anything about his situation, the only thing left for him to do, was to trust God. It seems as though God waits until the believer is finally ready to trust in Him; then He provides in a mighty way, so the believer will know, without a doubt, that it is from God. Duane had to trust God to provide, and as always, God was faithful to His Word!

Duane was out of work for about four months. This meant that he and his family had to live for four months on the equivalent of one month's wages. Most of us would think it couldn't be done, but at the end of those four months, they had taken only about $200 out of their savings. They should not have been able to do this. It should not have happened; but it did, because God provided in a mighty way!

On top of that, because Duane's job was a union job, he had to be 100% healed before he could return to work. In his type of work, there is no light duty work; therefore he had to be able do all the necessary lifting, or he couldn't return to work. The doctor would not give him a full release, until the end of January, 2012, but God intervened, and He returned to work in November, of 2011, three months early!

This never happens, and as far as Duane knows, he is the only one it has ever happened to. God changed the mind of Duane's supervisor, just like He changed the mind Pharaoh to let the Israelites go. A delivery route opened up, and Duane found himself driving back and forth to Glendive, Montana, doing a fraction of the lifting, but at the same pay! It meant that he had better hours, the same pay, and a fraction of the physical work that he had to do before!

God's Hand was all over this injury, where Duane was treated more than fairly. He had been quite foolish, when he was on vacation, with his handling of the ATV. He did not deserve to be back at work. But God is not fair, He is more than fair!

Duane's son, who was born 9 months and 5 days after that airplane crash, has been accepted to the United States Air Force Academy, in Colorado Springs, Colorado. He is the only high school student, from the eastern half of the state of Montana, to be accepted for the year of 2012!

Of all the twenty, or so, 2011 high school graduates from eastern Montana, who were nominated by their Senators or Representatives, Steven Neprud was the only one accepted! In addition to that, normally the academy would take in something like thirteen or fourteen hundred cadets, but 2012 was to be the smallest class ever, because of budget cuts!

Steven had worked diligently toward his goal of going to the Air Force Academy, since he was in the 7th grade. He spent his years in high school, preparing for that position. Although many boys seeking an appointment to the Air Force Academy generally take part in Civil Air Patrol or Boy Scouts, Steven did not. However, he did everything else, and he received his appointment. He also spent a lot of hours in prayer as did his parents and a lot of people around the country. Psalms 37:3-4 says, "Trust in the LORD and do good; dwell in the land and enjoy safe pasture. Delight yourself in the LORD and he will give you the desires of your heart".

Steven also applied to the Naval Academy and the Merchant Marine Academy, to spread out his options, just in case he was not accepted to the Air Force Academy. He received an appointment to the Merchant Marine Academy, in January of 2012, but he told them he would let them know as soon as he heard from the Air Force Academy. He missed an appointment to the Naval Academy, by about 200, and was put on the waiting list. Needless to say, God had a mighty hand in all of this!

Steven had been given an appointment to the Merchant Marine Academy, which meant that he would receive more than a two hundred thousand dollar education, paid for by the government! Yet Steven's heart was for an appointment to the Air Force Academy and he wanted to wait for that.

In the meantime, Satan brought doubts to the minds of his parents, as normally the appointments would have been out in January, but in 2011, they did not come out until March. Duane was wondering what to do about his vacation time. He wanted to be there for Steven, wherever he was going to be, but they still didn't know where that would be. So Duane dropped to his knees and put out a fleece, which means, he asked the Lord to give him a sign as to what to do. Five minutes later, the telephone rang and a fellow employee of his, asked him to change the time he had put in for his vacation! The vacation time he was asked to change *to* was the time when the Air Force Academy has Parents' Weekend! He would need to have that time off, if Steven was appointed to the Air Force Academy! Talk about a quick answer to prayer!

When Jesus was born, many miraculous things happened, and "Mary treasured up all these things and pondered them in her heart". (Luke 2:19) Duane and Larae have a lot to ponder in their hearts. They have a son that doctors had told them they would never have. God has had His hand on Steven all of his life, and he is going to a place a lot of young people just dream of. As Duane and Larae ponder the probability of all the things that have happened in their lives, they would say that the chances are far fewer than <u>one in a million</u>! With God, there are no coincidences, just non-confirmed miracles! I am also sure that Duane, Larae and Steven would all agree, that God is not fair, He is more than fair!

Things to Ponder

1. Looking back on your life what would have been the chances that you would have given your life over to Jesus on your own?
2. "The presence of the Holy Spirit filled the cab of the truck, to such an extent that He got Duane's total attention!" What has God used to get your attention?
3. At times God requires a step of faith before He moves. Has this happened in your life and if so how so?
4. "Duane was finally brought low enough, where he could not do anything about his situation, the only thing left for him to do, was to trust God." Has God ever had to bring you low for you to TRUST HIM?
5. What is the only thing the believer can do when Satan brings doubts to their minds? Have you ever had that happen to you?

18

Faith Builds Faith

One of the main reasons I wrote this book is because Faith builds Faith! If a person hears a story of faith, then he or she will have a little more faith, which will in turn create hope for the future. In fact, when I was praying one day, I asked God why he was having me write this book, since I am not a writer. All through school I avoided taking any English class that was not required, because it was something that I was not very good at. God responded and said, "So they will know."

The way things are, in this world, and in our country today, for that matter, I believe the Christian, or Believer, is going to need all the faith he or she can have, in order to be an overcomer. I believe each of us should tell others about all the things, both large and small, the Lord does in our lives. Also, those stories of faith draw people who do not know Jesus as Lord and Savior, to a point where they want to know more.

On February 6, 2012, I had a divine appointment to meet Becki Parisi of Harlowton, Montana. At 3:00 PM, I had made my usual trip to the Sportsman's Cafe, for coffee with a group of men, who met there every day. It was the birthday of one of the waitresses, so someone had provided cake for everyone, and I had a nice big piece. Soon I was not feeling very well, so I went home, vomited, and went to bed. By the time my wife, Linda, got home from work, I was in terrible pain, which resided in both my back, and the left side of my lower abdomen. Add to that, I was still vomiting, dehydrated and was also constipated.

The pain was so excruciating that Linda insisted I go to the Emergency Room, at the local hospital. The doctor on duty that evening, examined me and ordered a few tests. I had mentioned to him that I had diverticulitis. Sure enough, this was the problem, so he began to administer medication through an IV, and admitted me to the hospital for the night.

In the meantime, Linda called the prayer chain, asking for prayer for me.

The nurse that night was Becki Parisi, who came on duty for her shift, just about the time I was being admitted. Becki did not have a regular shift at the Harlowton hospital, but worked part time for several hospitals, in that part of the state of Montana. What were the chances that I would have an attack of diverticulitis, on the same day Becki was scheduled to work? Could it be a coincidence that Becki and I were at the same hospital, at the same time, and had never met before?

As you read, in the last chapter, 'With God there are no such things as coincidences; just non-confirmed miracles.' God has a purpose for everything he allows to come into the life of a believer, and Becki had a story that I needed to learn about, for this chapter of the book God called me to write. Antibiotics were administered to me, through the IV tube that was attached to my arm, and I was given a small amount of morphine for the pain.

As Becki took care of me that night, I immediately began to feel a lot better! Much better than I should have felt, from the small amount of morphine I had been given. As Becki and I began to visit, I knew that I was in that hospital bed for a purpose. The purpose was not because of the pain I had been feeling from the diverticulitis. It was because Becki had a story that I needed to hear; a story about faith building faith, which leads to hope! Becki was very busy, taking care of me and her other patients, in the Wheatland Memorial Hospital that night, and I had to wait about two months before I would hear the whole story, which follows:

Becki and her husband, Dennis, had made several mission trips in their lives, to a number of different countries. Most short term mission trips involve working with the local missionary, completing projects such as building, repairing, or painting. A short term mission trip might involve speaking in a local church, about what God has called that person to do. In 1996, Dennis and Becki felt called to return to Cambodia, but this was not to be a conventional mission trip.

After seeking the Lord through prayer, they felt He wanted them to go, walk, pray and to be His instruments of love to the people with whom they came in contact. It was to be a Holy Ghost mission trip, where they were to leave the planning open to the Lord, and just go wherever He told them to go. Doing that took a tremendous step of faith on their part, so they gathered together an intercessory prayer group in Harlowton. That prayer group was made up of believers who really knew how to pray.

Neither Dennis nor Becki had gone to any Bible School; they don't have any special titles or training. They are just ordinary people. But they are born again believers who really love God, and are willing to follow Him wherever He leads. God had called them to return to Cambodia, but this time to go to the center of the country. So they set out to Kampong Thom City which is the capital of Kampong Thom Province, in Cambodia.

Dennis and Becki are not wealthy people by any means; they are comfortable people, who love others with the love of God. On the other hand, they are very generous and at times like to be 'Santa Claus' to those in need, giving to help others live better lives. Their focus is always bringing the Gospel of Jesus Christ to this lost and dying world. Jesus says, "I am the way and the truth and the life. No one comes to the Father except through me". (John 14:6) Dennis and Becki emphasize, that everything they do is because of what Jesus has done for them.

As they travelled to Kampong Thom, they were prepared to use the resources that God had given them to help others. But the Lord told Dennis that they were not to give even a nickel away, they were to zip up their wallet. It is very difficult for someone who has the gift of generosity not to be generous, when he or she sees someone in need, but God had a different plan for meeting the needs of these people. Sometimes believers can get in God's way by trying to do everything on their own, instead of seeking out God's will in a situation. Dennis and Becki were mindful to see where God was leading them, so they put their wallets away.

They stayed in the home of a Cambodian man. He was actually an American citizen who had returned to Cambodia. He spoke English, so they were able to communicate through him. When they first arrived, they saw a small woman lying in a hammock. She appeared to be very ill. Her skin was very dry and leathery because she was so dehydrated.

They were asked to pray for this woman, but the people really wanted Dennis and Becki to give them $200 to take her to the hospital. She had been hit by a motorcycle, had a broken hip, and had not eaten for days. Her tongue was just like leather and she had internal injuries. Becki immediately recognized, from her nurses training, that this woman was near death, but God said to keep their wallets in their pockets.

Dennis and Becki knew that the only thing they could do was to pray, but Becki is a nurse and her medical knowledge fights against her faith. She had seen miracles in her life, but she didn't have that faith, for she knew how a dying person appears. However, Becki serves a God who is bigger than her medical knowledge, so she prayed.

Both Becki and Dennis knew that money was not an option, so they anointed the woman with oil and they prayed. As Dennis prayed, Becki laid her hand on that woman's belly. Then she prayed with compassion and mercy, pleading with the Lord to heal that lady. God was about to perform a miracle for which only He could receive the credit.

The next morning, when Becki came to breakfast, she saw a small woman squatting down as she entered the room. After Dennis and Becki had their meal, Becki turned to Dennis and told him that they needed to look in on the woman they had prayed for the night before. Dennis responded, "That woman just served us our breakfast, praise God!"

Becki had not recognized her, because she had changed so much from the night before. She no longer had that leathery look to her skin; she was up and about, serving Becki and Dennis as if nothing had happened! That miracle was so amazing that it gave an absolute rush to Becki, building her faith, and faith builds faith, which results in hope for tomorrow!

They had not done anything but obey the Lord in what He had told them. They had prayed with the little faith that they had, then the Holy Spirit showed up at that humble little house and performed a miracle! Faith builds faith, so the word got out that God was working through those two Americans, and what had started as a calm day turned into a very busy, fruitful day, as God moved through His people.

When the word got out, Dennis and Becki were asked to go to the home of a Pastor, whose wife had been hurt in a motorcycle accident. It seems that motorcycle accidents happen quite often. When they arrived at the Pastor's home, they found his wife was not well, at all. Her color was not good, her eyes were dazed, she had a severe headache, and she stumbled when she walked. She had a severe head injury and with Becki's medical knowledge, she knew that this woman needed to see a doctor, and she needed to see one soon!

On top of that, the Pastor loved his wife very much, and was very fearful for her. The Cambodian people generally think that Americans have money, and would be able to help that way. But God would have none of that! Again

Dennis and Becki had instructions from the Lord to keep their wallets closed, so they prayed a very simple prayer for God's healing. Instantly, God performed a miracle, and that Pastor's wife began laughing, and she looked like a completely different person!

Faith builds faith, which results in hope for tomorrow! Dennis and Becki jumped on the back of two different motorcycles and off they went, clinging desperately to the crazy-driving, Cambodian Pastors. They visited every outback village in the area, and the people brought their sick to be healed.

When people heard that Jesus was able to heal people of their sicknesses, they brought their sick friends and family to be healed. This is found in Mathew 15:29-31, which says,

> Jesus left there and went along the Sea of Galilee. Then he went up on a mountainside and sat down. Great crowds came to him, bringing the lame, the blind, the crippled, the mute and many others, and laid them at his feet; and he healed them. The people were amazed when they saw the mute speaking, the crippled made well, the lame walking and the blind seeing. And they praised the God of Israel.

Faith Builds Faith

Dennis and Becki were not the healers. Jesus was! He was just using them as His instruments of healing, as He did with the Apostles. In Acts 5:15-16, we find that

> people brought the sick into the streets and laid them on beds and mats so that at least Peter's shadow might fall on some of them as he passed by. Crowds gathered also from the towns around Jerusalem, bringing their sick and those tormented by evil spirits, and all of them were healed.

Jesus said, in John 14:12-14

> "I tell you the truth, anyone who has faith in me will do what I have been doing. He will do even greater things than these, because I am going to the Father. And I will do whatever you ask in my name, so that the Son may bring glory to the Father. You may ask me for anything in my name, and I will do it."

Some people believe that the gift of healing has passed away with time; I do not know about that. All I know for sure is, my God can do <u>anything</u>, and if He wanted to use

Dennis and Becki to heal people for His glory, then I say more power to Him! Faith builds faith which results in hope for the future, and those people now had hope! Dennis and Becki knew that what happened had nothing to do with them, and everything to do with the Lord Jesus. They were elated, to be used by God in such a way!

At one point, Dennis and Becki came upon a boy who was deranged, screaming and disrupting everything, just like the kind of thing that happened in the Gospels. It appeared as if that boy had demons controlling him. He had an amulet hanging around his neck, for there is a lot of superstition among those people. This boy was an orphan, and lived with his grandmother. As Becki and Dennis talked with her, the boy continued to disrupt them. They asked the grandmother, through the interpreters if she wanted the boy to be delivered, if she wanted him to be healed. When she finally said that she did, Dennis told the people to cut that thing off of the boy's neck.

The people brought an axe, and for a minute or so, Becki was afraid, because she didn't know if they were going to chop the boy's head off. All this was just a sign that those people needed to get serious about Jesus, forget their superstitions, and follow Jesus with all their hearts. They cut off that amulet while Dennis prayed a simple prayer. While that was happening, Becki struggled to hold the unruly boy, then all of a sudden the struggle was over. Becki sang Jesus Loves Me to him, as he fell asleep in her arms, totally delivered from the evil one. All through that time the people were so excited, seeing what the Lord was doing, that they forgot to eat!

The interpreter that Dennis and Becki had at that time, was not able to tell them everything that happened, so they just watched, as God showed up and healed many people! So many people responded, and God moved in a mighty way! One little girl who had a broken arm, was healed right before Becki's eyes. At one point, Becki asked herself if she was dreaming, or was this really happening?

Becki witnessed people being healed all around her, without the benefits of modern medicine. It truly was amazing. She was a nurse, trained in modern medicine, but she saw God heal without any doctors or nurses present. There were no surgeries performed, no pills, no pain killers, and no antibiotics. Just the Hand of God!

Dennis and Becki had survived three days of riding on the back of motorcycles, through the jungles of Cambodia. They had been used by God to heal numerous people, without the aid of modern medicine, and had seen the Hand of God at work! I am sure that they would agree that God is not fair, He is more than fair!

Things to Ponder

1. Have you ever had a divine appointment, where God used an unconventional way to get you there?
2. Dennis and Becki went on a "Holy Ghost" mission trip, where they were to leave the planning open to the Lord, and just go wherever He told them to go. How do you feel about this and would you be willing to do the same?
3. Becki is a nurse and her medical knowledge fights against her faith. What in your life fights against your faith?
4. "Faith builds faith, which results in hope for tomorrow!" What or who has God used to build your faith? Do you have hope for tomorrow?
5. Have you ever seen God heal without the use of "modern medicine"?

19

Only The Artist Knows

Years ago, my wife, Linda volunteered at a ministry in Bartlesville, Oklahoma. One day of each week, they have a devotional time for the staff and volunteers together, and Linda was there for it. The speaker was Willie Johnstone, an artist who does amazing things with chalk! He did a really unusual scenery picture. He had music playing as he drew, and he talked about the fact that no one except the artist knew what he was going to draw.

In his picture, Willie drew some mountains in the background, with a lake in the foreground. He had trees all around it, and it was a beautiful scene, as it all came together. As Willie drew, with the music playing, it was as if God

Only The Artist Knows

Himself was drawing the picture, on creation day. He had even put some flowers in the foreground, making it so real that everyone there was impressed.

Then just as everyone thought Willie was finished with the picture, he suddenly made three black marks across the picture. Immediately, most of the people thought he had ruined the picture, but Willie explained that the artist was not concerned about those black marks. The artist knows what the completed picture will look like, so with each black mark, he is not concerned, he can and will turn it into something beautiful!

Then he went on, to make a couple of the black marks into some aspen trees and the mark toward the top, near the middle of the picture, became an eagle, soaring high over the lake! Those black marks became things which added depth and character to the picture, making it even better than it was before he added the black marks.

God is the Artist and is painting a picture, in the lives of His creation. In the same way, God can and will make those black marks in our lives into something beautiful, if that person will just allow Him to. We, believers, get all upset when God allows certain things to come into our lives. These may appear as black marks to us, but God the Artist is not concerned. He can, and will, make them into something that He then will use to help someone else.

Instead, most believers expect that, when they give their lives over to Jesus, everything will be beautiful, and they will not have to deal with the problems of life anymore. That is just not so, but if the believer will trust God, He will turn those difficult times into something He can use.

My friend, Chuck Armstrong, of Billings, Montana, is a prime example of God taking the black marks in his life, and making them into something beautiful. He was brought up in a Christian home, as the son of a Pastor; that is, he was a preacher's kid. His father was a Pastor in the Assembly of God Church, in Oregon.

Chuck was saved when he was nine years old at summer camp, but later in life, he turned his back on God. As Chuck got older, he figured that he did not need God. Motorcycles were a big attraction to him, and for that matter, they still are to this day. He lived the stereo-typical biker lifestyle, which is the hard-core lifestyle. He was involved with drugs, heavy drinking, and motorcycle clubs. His life was filled with violence! He didn't work, but sold drugs, and ran around with women.

Chuck loved to fight all the time and he would beat people up, just for the fun of it. He got into a shootout, and found himself lying on a barroom floor, having been shot four times. A lot of people think they can wait until the last minute, before asking Jesus into their hearts, but for the most part, it doesn't work that way. Chuck was shot four times and was lying in a pool of his own blood! Yet, it never even crossed his mind, to get right with Jesus!

One might say that Chuck was living about as far away from God as he could get, but God still loved him. God must have been looking down on Chuck and thinking, "What have you gotten yourself into?" At the same time, God must have been hurting for Chuck. He loved Chuck so much, and wanted to minister to his hurting heart!

Chuck didn't want anything to do with God. So, if he saw someone from the Christian Motorcycle Association coming down the street, he would literally cross the street, in order to avoid them. He would not set foot inside a Church; to put it gently he was in total rebellion against God.

Family gatherings were not pretty. Chuck and his dad would be locked in an argument, within half of an hour. Chuck's dad constantly preached to him about his lifestyle, and Chuck just plain didn't want to hear it. At the same time,

Chuck had an irreverent, disrespectful attitude. He didn't care if he hurt his father's feelings or not. Chuck was a really bad apple, and he hurt the ones he should have loved the most!

One day, Chuck's sister had a talk with their father, telling him, that if he continued preaching to Chuck, he would just drive a bigger wedge between them, and close the doors of communication forever. She told their father all he had to do was to show Chuck love, so that is what he did! Their father and mother were prayer warriors, so they lifted Chuck before God all the time, and loved him right where he was, expecting nothing in return.

One of the greatest mistakes Christian parents make is trying to change their children on their own. Parents can tell their adult children all kinds of things that they need to change, but all anyone wants, is to feel loved. That is a hard thing to do, because most of the time parents want to fix what is wrong, so their children don't have to experience the pain that comes with bad choices.

The church needs to learn this lesson, as well. We need to love in the same way that Jesus loved us. He loves even the worst sinner with unconditional and extravagant love! He paid with His very life to make a way for us to be cleansed and made whole. We need to love people unconditionally, and with true hearts, and stop trying to change them. That's God's business!

Chuck moved to Billings, Montana, in 1990. There, in 1995, he met the woman who would become his wife. In 2000, Chuck's dad and mom made a trip to Billings, to perform the marriage ceremony for Chuck and his bride; it ended up being a biker's party. Chuck's dad did this out of love for his son, and Chuck's heart was beginning to soften, even though he did not know it.

In 2001, Chuck and his family went to visit his parents. Whenever they visited in the past, Chuck and his family would stay at the house, while his parents went to church. That Sunday was different, because Chuck decided, for some unknown reason, that they were going to church along with his parents. For the first time in many years, Chuck found himself sitting in a church, hearing the Word of God.

The next thing Chuck knew, his niece was asking him if he would go to church with her family too, since he had gone to church with his mom and dad. Chuck immediately told her, "Yes," and they travelled to Longview, Washington, to the Nazarene Church where his niece attended. Chuck's mom and dad went along too, instead of attending their own Church.

The service was a candlelight vigil, with Chuck sitting there nonchalantly, just like he belonged there — which he did! The preacher was delivering his message, when suddenly, God spoke to Chuck. In no uncertain terms, a loud voice said, "THIS IS YOUR LAST CHANCE." God was calling that lost sheep He had been searching for, for such a long time!

Chuck's response was a simple "Ok"! There must have been a joyous shout in heaven! In Luke 15:7, Jesus says, "I tell you that in the same way there will be more rejoicing in heaven over one sinner who repents than over ninety-nine righteous persons who do not need to repent". I believe there was a party in heaven, for God had just snatched Chuck from the hands of Satan, and Chuck's life would never be the same! "For this son of mine was dead and is alive again; he was lost and is found". (Luke 15:24)

The realization of what had happened did not come to Chuck for a couple of days, when he told his wife, Toni, that it was funny, but he had not cussed in two days! He continued that he did not want a drink, and had no yearnings for any drugs, which was an absolute miracle. Before that fateful day, he had been doing methamphetamines heavily and had been drinking every day.

Toni replied that she had noticed there was definitely something different about him! As they drove down the highway, Chuck told Toni that they needed to find a church to attend. "Okay," she agreed. She was up for the change which was happening in their lives. When they returned to Billings, they chose to start attending the East Gate Wesleyan Church, where Chuck's Dad had married them, a little over a year before!

How would the people of that church react to having a biker family in their midst? The church already knew a little about Chuck, because his step-daughter attended the Kid's Club program there. They knew from past experience, that they had to have that girl out the door at 8:00, or Chuck would be standing at the door yelling for her to come out. Would he be rejected by the church people, as he had rejected them, or would they accept him, in spite of his previous ways? So many Christians avoid everyone but the fellow Christians they know, but this Church welcomed them with open arms!

About a week after returning to Billings, Chuck came to the realization that God had taken away all of his addictions. Chuck had been around people who were addicted to drugs and alcohol, most of his adult life. He did not understand why God would take his addictions instantaneously, instead of easing him out of them. But later, he realized that God separated him from his previous lifestyle for about six months, so people could see the tremendous change in him!

Then God called Chuck back into the same motorcycle club he had been in before. Chuck told the club of his lifestyle change, that he was not the same person he had been before, and they just said, "Okay." Chuck became the national chaplain of the Ghost Rider Motorcycle Club! How ironic was that? First a bad boy in that motorcycle club, and then he was the national chaplain? Does God have a great sense of humor and a magnificent plan, or what?

If God had slowly eased Chuck out of the drugs and alcohol, Chuck would most likely not have returned to that same circle of people. Chuck now had no want, nor will, to do the stuff he had done before! The people he had run with before could see the difference God had made in his life!

People still look at Chuck, see the change and wonder about it. There are some who think that Chuck is faking it, or maybe he got in trouble with the law. The power of God in a person's life will always make people wonder. There will always be those who doubt the change is real. Mainly, that's because those people do not want to admit there is a God, who really cares about all of His creation, and that God loves even them!

At one point, Chuck went back to talk with the Pastor of that Nazarene Church in Longview, Washington, because the Pastor wanted to hear Chuck's testimony. After hearing what Chuck had to say, the pastor told Chuck that the message he gave wasn't a salvation message! To that, Chuck responded, "Maybe not for you but it was for me!" God doesn't need a pastor to preach. He can, and does speak directly, to anyone who is willing to listen. Chuck praises God for what He has done in his life, and in the life of his whole family!

For years, Chuck had avoided all contact with the Christian Motorcycle Association, but after turning his life over to God, he actually became a member of it for a time. Since then, the East Gate Wesleyan Church has formed a motorcycle ministry, in which Chuck became highly involved.

The East Gate Motorcycle Ministry has made several trips to Sturgis, South Dakota, for the Sturgis Motorcycle Rally. They have slept in the parking lot, and in the basement, of one of the Sturgis churches. They have walked up and down the street, witnessing to people. A lot of people have gotten angry with them. When a person lives a Godless life, he or she doesn't want God even mentioned; they don't want to hear it!

The sad thing is that they have suffered the anger of other Christian groups, because they were openly witnessing to those bikers. Those other Christians were offended, and that just isn't right. Christians need to learn that this is not a competition between different churches; but we are working for the same goal, of seeing the lost come to the Lord!

The worst thing anybody could have ever done to Chuck, before he gave his heart to the Lord, was to start witnessing to him. He had all the answers, he knew all about Jesus in his head and was ready with a comeback. He had learned scripture at an early age, and was ready to rebut anyone. For him it was easy, and he was really good at it!

Chuck has learned when God gives an opportunity, and is in control, he doesn't even need to start the conversation. He and others have learned that motorcycles are a tool to open lines of communication with bikers. If Chuck starts talking about someone's motorcycle, the owner of that motorcycle finds that Chuck is interested in him.

Then the motorcycle owner starts asking Chuck questions, which are not necessarily just about motorcycles, but are often questions about him. Those questions often lead to Chuck being able to share his testimony of God's work in his life.

On occasion, the motorcycle ministry gets a chance to pray for someone, and when that takes place, they ask that person what his or her need is, for the year. Then they ask God to bless him or her for the year, to guide his or her path, and to open up the direction that God wants him or her to go. They even pray for God to bless the use of the motorcycle for Him. That prayer becomes an open door, leading wherever God wants it to lead.

As Chuck shared his testimony with me, tears came to his eyes, as he remembered all that God had done for Him. One time, he asked his men's group to pray that he would be able to share without the tears. He had learned, in the outlaw motorcycle world that tears are a sign of weakness.

Then he was praying in public, and one of his friends said, "Wow. I never thought I'd see you pray, and I knew I'd never see you cry." He then said, "That tells me it's real." So now, he has a passion for Jesus Christ, and he is not ashamed of it. Tears show his emotion, telling the listener that, what he shares has had a tremendous effect on him.

I have concluded each chapter of this book with the statement "God is not fair. He is more than fair!" Chuck knows that as well as, if not better, than everyone else. Scripture says, in Romans 3:23, "all have sinned and fall short of the glory of God". It also says, in Romans 6:23, "For the wages of sin is death, but the gift of God is eternal life in Christ Jesus our Lord". Chuck knows that he had sinned and deserved to spend eternity in hell. That is fair, that is what he deserved.

Notice the second part of that verse, "but the gift of God is eternal life in Christ Jesus our Lord". (Romans 6:23) God has made a way that anyone can avoid spending eternity in hell, and that is because He is more than fair!

If you are reading this, and want what Chuck, and so many others have, then I want you to know that you, too, can have it! God is so much more than fair in that He loves you, no matter what you have done in your life. He is so much more than fair in that there is nothing you have done, or can do, that would stop Him from loving you! All that He asks is that you choose to follow him; it's up to you!

Scripture says, in Romans 10:9, "That if you confess with your mouth, 'Jesus is Lord,' and believe in your heart that God raised him from the dead, you will be saved". All you have to do is ask Jesus to come into your heart, and be Lord of your life. He will clean you up, as you walk daily with Him. I would also encourage you to find yourself a church home, where the body of believers can disciple you in your walk with Jesus.

If you asked Jesus into your heart, or recommitted your life to Him, I would love to hear about it! If God has done some other "more than fair" thing in your life, I would love to hear about that, as well! Please contact me at lepollock@cableone.net and tell me your story.

Things to Ponder

1. God is not concerned about those black marks in your life, because He can make them into something beautiful. What are some of the black marks you would like to see Him make beautiful?
2. Most believers expect that, when they give their lives over to Jesus, everything will be beautiful, but that just is not so. How do you feel about that statement?
3. Chuck went out of his way to avoid Christians. What can believers (Christians) do to help others to not avoid them?
4. "Chuck has learned when God gives an opportunity, and is in control, he doesn't even need to start the conversation. He and others have learned that motorcycles are a tool to open lines of communication with bikers." What do you have that God could use to open the doors of communication between you and unbelievers?
5. "God is so much more than fair in that He loves you, no matter what you have done in your life. He is so much more than fair in that there is nothing you have done, or can do, that would stop Him from loving

you!" How do you feel when you read this? Go and share the love of Jesus with the world!!!

CPSIA information can be obtained at www.ICGtesting.com
Printed in the USA
LVOW13s0959221013

358032LV00001B/90/P

MURDER AT THE EMPIRE

AN EVER AFTER MYSTERY

CATHE SWANSON

Copyright © 2021 by Cathe Swanson

All rights reserved.

No part of this book may be reproduced in any form or by any electronic or mechanical means, including information storage and retrieval systems, without written permission from the author, except for the use of brief quotations in a book review.

ISBN: 978-1-951839-36-9

Celebrate Lit Publishing

304 S. Jones Blvd #754

Las Vegas, NV, 89107

http://www.celebratelitpublishing.com/